The Whale Whisperer

By:

Mustafa A. Nejem

The Whale Whisperer
Copyright © 2023 by Mustafa A. Nejem

Lost in waves, found in sea creatures.

Table of Contents

Chapter 01

A WHISPER ON THE WIND
A Strange Ability

Zoe sighed as she gazed out at the ocean, waves crashing against the rocky shore. The seagulls cried above as always, but today she felt like something was calling to her, a whisper on the wind she couldn't explain.

Ever since she was little, Zoe felt drawn to the sea. As soon as she learned to walk, she would toddle down to the beach and spend hours watching the tides roll in and out. But it was more than just a love of the ocean - sometimes she swore she could hear voices beneath the surface, songs and sounds that soothed her soul.

Her parents didn't understand. They thought she had an active imagination, that she was projecting human characteristics onto animal noises. But Zoe knew what she heard was real. The scientists she mentioned it to just patronized her, indulging her dreams without really listening. No one believed her strange connection was possible.

That morning, as soon as she woke, Zoe felt an urgency she'd never experienced before. She rushed out of her small beachside home and raced down the sand, bare feet padding over shells and stones. When she reached the shoreline, waves lapping at her ankles, Zoe took a deep breath and closed her eyes.

And then she heard it - a faint chorus of clicking and whistling, carrying clearly across the miles of open ocean. It was a sound she'd heard in her dreams but never with such clarity. Zoe's eyes flew open in shock. Someone...no, some creatures, were calling out to her, begging for help in the only way they knew how.

"I know you're out there," she whispered to the sea. "I can hear your song. What is it you need?"

The clicking grew louder, more insistent, mixed with low moans of distress. Zoe could sense the fear and desperation behind the sounds, and her heart ached in empathy. She wished more than anything she could understand what they were saying in words rather than just interpreting their emotional cues.

The voice seemed to be coming from the north, out past the shoreline reefs where the water grew deep. Zoe glanced behind her at the empty beach - no one else was around to witness her having a one-sided conversation with the waves. But she knew without a doubt she wasn't imagining things. This call had come directly to her.

Zoe cupped her hands around her mouth. "I'm here to help! Keep singing to me - I'll follow your song." With that, she turned and raced back to her house, sandals flying. There was no time to waste.

She burst through the front door, startling her mother who was washing dishes. "They're in trouble!" Zoe gasped. "Out past the reef, I have to go now!"

Her mother stared at her in confusion. "Zoe, slow down - who's in trouble? What are you talking about?"

"The whales," Zoe panted, trying to catch her breath. "I can hear them calling for help. They need me, Mom, please!"

A look of concern came over her mother's face, mixed with a resigned sort of sadness. "Oh Zoe..." she said gently. "Not this again. You know whales can't actually talk to humans."

"But they CAN talk to ME!" Zoe shouted in frustration. She didn't have time to argue theories - every second could mean life or death in the open ocean for whoever had reached out. "Please, you have to believe me! I'll prove it, just lend me a boat."

Her mother hesitated, clearly torn between dismissing Zoe's claims like always, and risking encouraging her fantasy if it turned out to just be the wind after all. But one look at Zoe's pleading eyes, shining with conviction, made the decision.

"Alright," she said with a sigh. "But I'm coming with you. If we don't find anything within the hour, that's it, okay?"

Zoe nodded rapidly. "Deal! Thank you, thank you!" She ran to hug her mother, and within minutes they were loading up their small motorboat with supplies just in case. Zoe wasn't sure what they might find, but she had to be prepared to help however she could.

As they pushed off from the shore and puttered out toward the open ocean, Zoe closed her eyes again and focused on listening. The clicking was growing fainter - were they moving further away? She cupped her hands around her mouth. "I'm coming, just keep singing!" she called out to the whales.

Her mother glanced over; one eyebrow raised. But before she could say anything, Zoe held up a hand. "Shh...do you hear it?" The song was growing louder once more, as if in response. Zoe spun toward the sounds, leaning over the side of the little boat. "That way - north by northwest. Step on it!"

They sped off across the waves, Zoe straining her senses to make sure they stayed on course. After about 20 minutes, a new noise began to emerge from beneath the clicks and whistles - low moans that sent shivers down Zoe's spine. Anxiety, distress... she could feel the emotions through the singing.

"There!" Zoe shouted, pointing ahead. Two tall fins sliced through the surface in the distance, swishing from side to side. As her mother steered closer, more dorsal fins appeared, seeming to circle aimlessly.

Zoe's heart soared. "Humpback whales! Look how many of them there are, there must be over 20." She climbed up onto the bow of the boat to get a better view.

The pod was in disarray, whales swimming erratically instead of in their normal tight-knit formation. Several had nasty wounds marring their glistening skin. But it was the smallest whale that caught Zoe's attention - a young calf, barely half the size of the others, that seemed unable to keep up and was falling behind the group. Its cries were weak and pathetic.

Anger and empathy swelled in Zoe's chest. Someone had hurt these gentle giants, and they were paying the ultimate price. She cupped her hands around her mouth once more. "It's okay, I'm here now. I'll help you," she called out over the waves.

The singing grew louder and more agitated, as if the whales didn't quite believe someone could understand them after all. Zoe waited, breath held, then cheered as one huge whale broke away from the others and swam right up to the boat, peering at her with one wild eye the size of her torso.

His song was soft and low now, almost apologetic, as if begging for forgiveness that she'd had to come so far. Zoe smiled through her tears. "It's not your fault. Now let me help - where are they hurting you?"

The large whale let out a mournful cry and turned, fins cutting through the water as he swam back to the pod. Zoe eagerly followed in the boat, hovering on the edge of the group as various whales surfaced and exhaled, blown fog spraying across the surface.

Then she saw it - long lines of red floating in the water beneath them, delicate ribbons unfurling like bloody banners. Her stomach lurched as she realized the telltale marks were from whale snares, floating nets designed to entangle and drown.

"Poachers," Zoe hissed through gritted teeth. No wonder the pod was in such disarray - they were fighting to free themselves while injured and exhausted. She turned to her still stunned mother behind the wheel. "Call the Coast Guard right away, they need help!"

As her mother got on the radio, begging for an immediate response, Zoe did her best to soothe and assess the whales. Several had deep cuts from thrashing against the cruel nets, while others looked weakened from blood loss and lack of food as they spent days trapped below.

But what worried Zoe most was the small calf - he had managed to wriggle free, but a long coil of net still dragged behind him, weighed down by seaweed and debris. His tiny flukes slapped uselessly at the surface as he struggled to keep up, and with each breath he let out a weak, gasping cry.

"Shhh, it's okay," Zoe crooned softly as she pulled herself out along the bow, reaching a hand into the water just inches from his massive eye. "I'm going to help you. Mom, get me a knife - hurry!"

With trembling hands, Zoe accepted the blade from her mother and leaned out over the side. The calf watched her curiously even through his panic and exhaustion. "This might sting a little, but it will feel better soon, I promise," she said in what she hoped was a soothing tone.

Then, carefully and gently, she began sawing away at the netting wrapped around his tail, unwinding the coils bit by grueling bit. The calf let out a few pitiful squeals as fibers pulled at his tender skin, but he didn't struggle or try to flee, seeming to understand she meant to help rather than harm.

It took nearly 20 minutes of sawing, pulling, and untangling, but finally the last piece of net fell away into the water. Zoe slumped back in relief, sweat dripping down her face, as the calf suddenly surged forward with renewed vigor. He let out a series of joyful, clicking cries, breaching out of the water just feet from the boat in the wildest display of thanks and celebration.

"You're very welcome, sweet boy," Zoe laughed, wiping her eyes. The other whales began singing too then, as if in a choral chorus of praise and gratitude. Her mother squeezed her shoulders from behind, smiling through her own tears at the tender sight of human and whale bonding before them.

"I didn't believe you at first, Zoe," her mother admitted. "But I see it now. You do have a gift - and these beautiful creatures understand you in a way no one else does."Before Zoe could reply, the sounds of approaching sirens cut through the air. She waved wildly as the Coast Guard boats pulled up; officers shocked by the grisly scene that met their eyes. "The poachers - they were here, and some whales are still trapped!" Zoe cried, pointing to the shreds of netting still tangling fins and tails below.

"Get those divers in the water now, we have to save as many as we can before it's too late," the lead officer barked into his radio. Zoe clutched her mother's hand tightly, willing the rescuers to work fast against the fading daylight. Lives hung in the balance - not just whale lives, but also Zoe's belief that people could understand each other across all seeming boundaries if they only took the time to listen.

The rescue divers dove swiftly into the waves, slicing through the crimson-tinged water with knives in hand. Zoe watched tensely from the boat as silhouettes moved back and forth below the surface, tending to the whales one by one.

A few of the divers emerged carrying remnants of netting, throwing them into a disposal pile with disgust. But many more returns were accompanied by joyous whistles and clicks from freed whales. Slowly but surely, the pod was regaining its shape as its members were released from their bonds.

When at last no more divers surfaced with slashing tools, Zoe let out the breath she'd been holding. Most of the whales now swam strongly together in a tight-knit cluster, singing songs of thanks. Only a couple continued to lag behind with injuries too severe for field treatment.

"We'll need to transport those two in for specialized care," the Coast Guard captain said grimly, peering through binoculars. "And I want this whole area searched top to bottom for anymore traps or debris. These were definitely set intentionally."

Zoe's eyes blazed with fury. "Then we have to find the ones responsible. These whales won't be safe until the poachers are caught." Her mother squeezed her shoulder reassuringly even as fear flashed across her face - she knew all too well her daughter's determination once her protective instincts kicked in.

"Leave that part to us, miss," the captain replied firmly. "You've done your heroic duty for the day. I suggest getting home and resting - it's been quite an ordeal." Still, he couldn't help but shoot Zoe an admiring smile. "Not every day we get a whale whisperer lending a hand. These fellas sure seem grateful to have you on their side."

Zoe smiled, rubbing the side of the calf who had swum over to nuzzle her hand. His injuries were healing but he seemed loathe to part from his rescuer just yet. "I'm just glad I could understand them calling for help. Next time, maybe it won't take me so long to get here."

Her mother's brows knit with concern. "Let's hope there isn't a next time, sweetie." She steered their boat away from the milling pod as divers began loading the most badly hurt whales onto transport floats. But even as they pulled away, Zoe couldn't tear her eyes from the immense creatures waving their flukes and singing out across the water.

A deep bond had formed between her and these whales - she felt their relief, their joy, their protectiveness toward each other. And she knew, without fully comprehending how yet, that their lives were forever intertwined. Wherever the pod went, Zoe would follow, determined to be their advocate and guardian against those who sought to harm them. This was only the beginning.

As Zoe watched the whales' fins fade into the distance, she felt a tug of longing to stay with them and make sure they were truly safe. But her mother was right - it had been an exhausting day and the coming night would only bring more uncertainty.

The ride home passed in a blur as Zoe replayed the day's events in her mind. She couldn't believe this morning she had merely been another girl daydreaming by the sea, and now whales actually communicated with her as an equal. A sense of purpose swelled in her chest at the thought of all she might accomplish for them.

When they pulled into dock, Zoe was surprised to see a small crowd had gathered on the shore. Her neighbors began cheering and clapping as she climbed out of the boat on unsteady legs, still processing everything that transpired.

"We heard what happened on the radio," said Mrs. Sanchez, squeezing Zoe's hand proudly. "Our little town hero! You saved those whales all on your own."

Zoe blushed at the praise but stood taller. "I was just listening like I always do. The whales called out for help and I had to answer."

A familiar scientist shouldered his way to the front, grinning down at her. "Well, young lady, it seems you've proven your gift is real after all. I'd be a fool not to take you seriously from here on." He patted Zoe's shoulder gently. "If you'll allow me, I'd like to study you - learn more about how this connection works. It could help whales worldwide."

Zoe lit up at the prospect of being believed for once, of helping the whales through scientific means rather than skepticism. She nodded eagerly, feeling the first stirrings of the activist she was destined to become. This was only the start of her mission to protect the oceans' gentle songsters.

Saying quick goodbyes to the well-wishers, Zoe followed her mother home, waves still singing faintly in her mind. As the sunset blazed orange and purple on the water, she knew this day had changed everything. Her calling had been proven, and from now on she would dedicate her life to being the voice of whales wherever they needed saving. Her whisperings had been heard at last.

VOICES UNDER THE SEA

Zoe woke just before dawn, the whispering whales from her dreams echoing in her mind. She rose and dressed quietly so as not to wake her mother, eating a quick breakfast as the first glimpses of orange sunk below the horizon.

Grabbing her binoculars and a bag with supplies, Zoe slipped out the front door and headed down to the shore. The sun was just appearing over the ripples as she scanned the waves eagerly, hoping to catch sight of the pod from yesterday.

At first, all seemed calm and still. A few seagulls circled overhead hunting for breakfast while crabs scuttled along the rock tidepools. But then, far out on the northern reaches, Zoe spotted the recognizable spray of a whale breach.

She lifted her binoculars to get a better view. Sure enough, the familiar circular grouping of dorsal fins was gliding just below the surface, an intricate choreographed dance of singing, diving whales. Zoe estimated there were at least 40 in total in the tight-knit clan.

As she watched, a small dark shape emerged from the water and lingered at the surface, flapping its fins energetically. Even at this distance, Zoe knew it was her little calf friend from yesterday, waving as if he had sensed her watching eyes upon them.

She waved back even though he couldn't see it, filled with joy to see him thriving after his ordeal. But her smile soon faded as another shape rose into focus behind the pod - a flashy speedboat zooming toward the vulnerable group much too fast.

Zoe gasped, worry flooding her heart. What if these people meant the whales harm? She had to get out there, had to protect them. Without a second thought, she raced to the dock and untied her family's small motorboat, leaping inside and cranking the engine desperately.

As the little boat putted through the waves as quickly as it could, Zoe watched the scene unfolding with dread. The pod's elegant ballet broke down into distress as they sensed danger approaching, cries of alarm and fear rippling outward. She had to believe she could get there in time.

Zoe urged her boat faster through the waves, but the speedboat was gaining rapidly on the panicking pod. She knew whales could hardly outswim such a craft in open waters. Thinking fast, Zoe grabbed her phone and dialed the number for the marine research center.

"Please, you have to help!" she shouted to the scientist who answered. "The poachers are back - I see them chasing the pod from yesterday. Send help immediately!"

As she hung up and focused back on the scene, Zoe's heart sank. The boats were almost upon the whales now, closing in from both sides in a threatening encirclement. One man stood on the prow with a rifle in hand, while the others in the boat jeered and hounded the pod into a tight cluster.

Zoe was still too far to make out faces, but she would never forget those ruthless men who left the whales for dead the first time. Screaming wordlessly in fury, she gunned her little boat as fast as its engine could strain.

Just as the man lifted his rifle to take aim at the nearest whale, Zoe stood up and started waving her arms wildly. "HEY!" she bellowed at the top of her lungs. "Leave them alone!"

Whether it was her distraction or the pod's sudden luck, none of the bullets found their mark that time. But the poachers had still achieved their purpose - the whales were trapped between the two boats in a state of panic. Zoe knew if she didn't disrupt them soon, the scene would end in a bloodbath.

As she raced nearer, Zoe desperately cast about for a plan. Her eyes fell on the supply bag at her feet, and sudden inspiration struck. She grabbed a can of kerosene left over from a camping trip and started splashing it through the air behind her boat, drawing zigzagging streaks across the ocean.

"MOM, LIGHT IT!" Zoe yelled into her phone where her mother was on the line, having answered groggily to the early call. Within moments, a sputtering line of orange flames blazed across the water, acting as a flammable barricade between the whales and danger.

The poachers bellowed curses as the wall of fire separated them from their prey. But Zoe had succeeded in her goal - the pod was now safely on her side, and she maneuvered her boat between them and the menacing speedboat.

"Leave now and I won't call the Coast Guard," Zoe shouted, hands clenched white around the steering wheel in attempt to mask her shaking. She prayed her blunt threat would work to stall them until help arrived.

For a tense moment, no one moved, the air filled with the crackling of flames and cries of distressed whales. Then one of the poachers spit over the side in Zoe's direction before spinning their boat around with a roar of the engine.

"This ain't over, little girl. You and those whales will pay," he growled as they sped away across the waves. Zoe didn't let out her breath until they were just a speck on the horizon, too far to turn back from.

Wiping her sweaty palms, Zoe turned to soothe the pod. The flames were already dying out, but ropes of acrid smoke still hung in the air, adding to the whales' panic. She began crooning to them softly, as calm and comforting as she could muster.

"It's alright, you're safe now. I promise I won't let anyone hurt you." Slowly, their singing responded in kind, the tight cluster loosening bit by bit as trust was regained. A few even swam over tentatively to nuzzle Zoe's boat in thanks.

Still trembling, Zoe couldn't help but laugh and cry at the same time while embracing their glistening faces. The pod's bond with her gave her courage beyond imagining, and in that moment, she knew she would follow them to the ends of the earth.

By now the fire had dissipated completely, leaving an ashy slick across the waves. Zoe scanned the horizon hopefully for the research boats, knowing backup was crucial after issuing such a direct threat. Soon familiar forms appeared in the distance.

Relief swelled as the marine experts arrived, already aware of the situation from Zoe's call. At last, she could rest, content the pod was safely in protective hands once more - though she doubted this would be the end of their battles. The poachers' words echoed darkly in her mind.

As the marine researchers assessed the whales for any injuries, Zoe recounted the harrowing ordeal to the lead scientist. His frown deepened with concern.

"This is a far more organized operation than we feared. Poaching rings don't give up easily once challenged." He squeezed Zoe's shoulder reassuringly. "But you've proven yourself a fierce defender of these whales. With your help and insight, I believe we can catch these criminals."

Zoe took a steadying breath, squaring her shoulders. "I'll do whatever it takes to bring them down and keep this pod safe. The poachers said we'll pay - well, they're not getting away with threats."

A few of the braver whales had circled back, drawn to Zoe's familiar presence. She stroked their smooth sides, drawing strength from their tranquil song rising again after the morning's terror.

"We'll beat them together," she vowed to the pod. Her words were for them, but also a self-promise - that with each challenge, her resolve would only grow stronger on behalf of her ocean family. They had chosen her as their protector, and she would not fail that trust.

In the following weeks, Zoe and the researchers worked tirelessly gathering intel. She spent hours with the whales, learning their songs, behaviors and migratory patterns and relaying what she observed. Piece by piece the bigger picture emerged.

Satellite tags were applied to track movements, while Zoe continued befriending individual whales to assist with identifies should any go missing. Though she ached to stay in the ocean forever, nightly swims recharging her before each new dawn's efforts.

Finally, after pinpointing key locations and signs, they struck gold - hidden boats laden with illegal fishing gear, trace evidence in specialized labs, and most damning, recordings of poachers bragging about "those singing whales" easily snared offshore.

The team had their suspects. Now it was time for justice. But would it come before more innocent lives were lost? Zoe could only pray the pod's defenders were ready for whatever may come. Their foes had proven ruthless - and the stakes had never been higher.

With the evidence gathered, Zoe accompanied the researchers to the local authorities with the poaching case. As they poured over incriminating photos and recordings, the grim-faced officers seemed at last convinced of the magnitude they faced.

"Rounding up an entire organized ring won't be easy, but we'll do everything in our power," the police chief promised. Zoe tried to feel reassured, though anxiety still churned in her gut. Such ruthless criminals were not likely to go down without a fight.

In the following weeks, patrols increased massively throughout known whaling waters. But it seemed the poachers had gone underground, concealing their operations expertly to evade capture. Each dead end only wound Zoe tighter with stress.

She doubled her efforts with the pod, ensuring no injuries or strange behaviors went unnoted that could provide clues. The whales seemed to sense her concern, radiating calm reassurance through their songs as they swam together.

Yet one morning, Zoe's fears were realized - she arrived to find the pod milling about without purpose, crying plaintively. A head count proved five had vanished overnight without a trace. Zoe broke down sobbing, blaming herself for failing them.

Through her tears, she felt a nudge - her calf friend pressed against her with a soft, sad croon. Lifting her eyes, Zoe glimpsed new strength and fire within the pod. They would grieve, but not be defeated...and their bond with this young human ran deeper than any foe.

"We'll find them, I promise," Zoe vowed with renewed ferocity. Her gift had brought them this far, and she would push its limits until every last whale was delivered from danger. That night, she swam far from shore and closed her eyes, opening her mind more than ever before to the whales' songs drifting on the current.

When Zoe emerged from the water at dawn, her eyes held a wild new light that had the researchers exchanging nervous glances. "I know where they're keeping the missing whales. Get the authorities - it's time to end this, once and for all."

Zoe led the task force of police boats out to a remote stretch of coastline she and the whales had shown her. As they approached under radio silence, a rundown marine warehouse came into view, armed guards posted outside.

She signaled to cut engines, and they drifted the last hundred yards silently until they could hear distressed singing coming from within. Zoe knew with gut-wrenching certainty - the stolen whales were inside.

"Surround the building," the chief ordered softly. "Move in on my command." Zoe gripped the railing, heart in her throat as teams stealthily took positions. This was it - if they failed, those whales would be lost forever.

At the chief's signal, sirens blared to life and officers spilled from the boats with weapons raised. For a moment, no one moved as the poachers stared in disbelief. Then pandemonium erupted as they scrambled for their rifles and speedboats.

Zoe chased after two men fleeing around back, rage and adrenaline powering her slight frame. She tackled one around the legs, wrestling his gun away just as a shot rang out. Officers engages in their own clashes up ahead.

Struggling fiercely, Zoe managed to pin the man long enough for backup to swarm and restrain him in cuffs. Shaking, she examined the second prone form a few yards away - the chief standing over a still body, gun-smoke curling from his weapon.

"He fired first," the chief said heavily. "It was him or my men." Zoe nodded, turning quickly to scan for more threats even as her insides roiled. The second man was arrested without further violence, leaving an eerie quiet.

Together they rushed inside, Zoe's gasp echoing off metal walls at the scene. Five humpbacks were chained tightly in a small tank, skins rubbed raw, eyes wild with fear. But she raced to the edge, crooning in their dialect until the nearest responded with joyful clicking.

"It's okay, Papa - I'm here now. We'll get you out," she soothed through tears. The chief radioed for transport, while Zoe and officers began the laborious work of freeing the trapped giants, slice by careful slice.

By nightfall, the last whale was released, rejoining a jubilant pod outside as justice was served onshore. Zoe sighed in utter relief and exhaustion, leaning against her calf friend's side as the sun sank behind them all. At long last, the singing whales were safe.

FIRST CONTACT

With the poaching ring dismantled at last, a fragile peace settled over the whale pod and the coastal community. Zoe spent long days swimming and bonding, ensuring each scar—whether physical or emotional—was healing.

The pod thrived alongside their human friend, learning to see all people with less fear thanks to Zoe's gentle guidance. Though dangers surely remained, for now the ocean sang with relief and songs of gratitude.

One glistening morning, Zoe awoke before dawn as usual to greet the new day. But something pulled her from shore earlier than ever, an inexplicable tug deep in her soul. As she watched the dark sea from the cliffs, faint whispers brushed her mind.

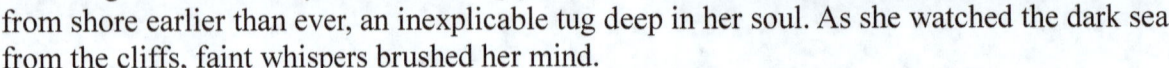

Zoe plunged into the waves, swimming further than she ever had from land alone under moonlight. Her breath caught at two mysterious shapes gliding toward her through the dim current, enormous yet graceful.

They surfaced just feet away, towering forms that took Zoe's breath away. Not humpbacks— sleek bodies mottled blue-gray, heads smooth and tapered, blows streaming from two blowholes. Orcas had come at her call, and she knew.

Reaching out with all her heart, Zoe greeted the great orcas in the language of the deep, as natural as breathing. Their songs flooded back, welcoming yet cautious, tinged with flecks of fear and questions. But mostly—curiosity toward this strange singing human.

Zoe assured them of her gentle intent, telling of the pod she watched over and protected. Her heart swelled as understanding dawned between them, barriers melting away in the dark waters. These orcas had heard whispers too, drawn by the call of a kindred spirit between worlds.

As dawn lit the rippling sea, Zoe bid her new friends farewell with a promise—that together, their voices would spread a message of hope across all the waves. Change was coming to heal old wounds, and unite all people of the oceans in harmony. Her mission had only begun.

Zoe returned to shore energized by her encounter, but also brimming with new questions. She and the orcas had communicated on a deeper level than even with the humpbacks, sensing vast amounts of untouched potential in their connection.

As she floated in the research center's outdoor tank that afternoon helping with medical checks on the pod, Zoe described the magical meeting to Papa Whale listening intently beside her. His answering song was thoughtful, suggesting orcas and humans had a long shared history deserving of respect.

One of the scientists overheard, looking up with interest. "There haven't been resident orca pods sighted this far south in decades. Their cultures were devastated by captures for shows. But it seems they're exploring old territories again."

Her mind whirled with possibilities. That night, Zoe immersed herself in every archived tale of human/orca relations she could find online and in books. Once seen as fierce competitors, some First Nations had lived in balance with the 'people of the sea' for generations.

The orcas were intelligent, family-oriented and knowledgeable beyond imagination about the oceans. Perhaps it was time for a new chapter of cooperation to begin, guided by understanding on both sides. Zoe knew that to truly honor her call as a voice for all whales meant walking a path of reconciliation.

In the coming days, she returned to her nightly meditations, spirit open as ever to any visitors wishing to communicate. Sure enough, one moonlit swim she found herself joined once more by her new orca friends, this time with more of their pod.

As their songs wove together in the gentle current, Zoe felt plans forming—ideas to educate people about orcas' complexity and start mending ancient seafaring bonds. But first, she and the orcas had farther to travel down this road of discovery themselves.

"Teach me of your world, as I share what I've learned of mine," Zoe requested into the listening dark. Two massive pods were coming together, and from their combined voices would spring new life for all the ocean's children. This was only the start.

And so began Zoe's amazing journey of learning from the orcas themselves. Night after night, she swam among their fluid elegance beneath the stars, listening raptly as they shared tales of ancient memory and wisdom.

She observed the intricate social structures of family pods, the hunting techniques passed down through generations, songs carrying information across vast distances. The orcas' intelligence left her in awe, seeing the ocean through their perceptive eyes.

In turn, Zoe taught them about the changes wrought upon the seas since the last orca voices echoed here. She showed photographs and explained human activities, from fishing and shipping to growing conservation efforts.

While some practices gave the orcas pause, they seemed glad to hear of people now protecting rather than fearing them. Through it all flowed a current of hope - that as the whales had accepted Zoe, humans too might learn if given truth and understanding.

Word began to spread among the local orcas of the special human in their midst. More and more joined Zoe's nightly lessons, and she greeted each new face with joy. Their songs carried her message far on the wind, in exchange bringing news of distant cousins and waters yet unseen.

Before long, a local film crew caught wind of the unprecedented meetings. With the orcas' permission, Zoe began working with them to capture footage for an educational documentary. She hoped it would dazzle people with the orcas' sentience and spark a love for protecting them.

At the documentary's premiere, the theater fell utterly silent, then erupted into amazed applause. Zoe swelled with pride seeing these majestic beings in a new light. At the after party, a famous conservationist approached - "You've done something incredible here. The orcas need a voice, and you may be the one to give it to the world."

Her mission had only begun. But thanks to the orcas' trust and guidance, Zoe felt ready to share their song with all who would hear. Their voices would rise together across the waves, carrying a message to heal both ocean and soul.

***

Chapter 02

A CRY FOR HELP

POACHERS ON THE HUNT

It had been six months since Zoe helped expose the ruthless whaling ring and bring safety to the pod. In that time, she had learned so much from the whales and orcas, while working tirelessly to spread their message far and wide.

Thanks to Zoe's documentary and public outreach, support was growing nationwide for stronger protections of local waters. She received invitations from aquariums and universities to share her incredible gift. But Zoe's heart remained with the pods, and for now the small coastal town felt right.

One blustery autumn morning, Zoe awoke to find the whole pod in an unusual state of upset. Their songs told of unfamiliar boat sounds disturbing their migratory route overnight. A quick call to the research center confirmed no scheduled activities.

Unease prickled Zoe's skin as she hurried to meet them. When no obvious injuries were found, she dove in for a closer communication. The whales' anxiety was palpable - whatever disturbed their travel held darkness in its wake that echoed of past terrors.

Zoe assured them all was well now, but inside fear gnawed that old adversaries may have returned despite their victory. She had grown complacent, failing to heed lingering warnings. From that day, extra patrols and satellite monitoring were arranged once more as a precaution.

Weeks passed uneventfully as autumn faded to winter's chill. Then one frigid morning, the research center received a panicked SOS - fishermen had come across an abandoned whaling vessel adrift at sea, its hold filled with telltale crimson. Zoe's heart seized at the implications.

Racing to the docks, Zoe felt her fears confirmed at the grim expressions awaiting her onboard the trawler. In the dark hold lay a scene from nightmares - flesh and blubber stripped messily from whale bones, as if the killers had been disturbed.

"It's them - it has to be the same ring," Zoe said hollowly, recalling all too vividly the last such horrors. The scientist nodded gravely. "All signs point to it. And this time, they seem to be expanding their reach."

Whirling, Zoe made call after desperate call but reached no reassuring pod songs in response. She refused to accept the finality yawning inside, urging the trawler to full speed toward the whales' usual route. If they could be found alive.

Hours passed in agony until a faint echo reached Zoe's straining senses - the weakest calling of souls in deep peril. "There!" she cried, and they hurtled toward a scene of chaos on the waves.

A massive whaling ship loomed beyond, harpoon guns ready, as two smaller speedboats herded a panicked remnant of the pod. Zoe watched in horror as flashing steel struck home, dragging a silenced whale to gruesome slaughter.

"Stop them, please!" she screamed at the fishermen, who wasted no time radioing the Coast Guard. But response would be too slow - these whales had minutes left at most. Thinking fast, Zoe unstrapped one of the abandoned floats from the trawler.

Grabbing a flashlight and marine radio, she tapped into an inner bravery swimming had taught her long ago. "I'll distract them. Ram the float into their propellers when I say." With that, she leapt into the raging sea and kicked toward the doomed pod.

The icy water stole Zoe's breath, but she forced herself to keep swimming towards the frantic scene. As the poachers spotted her tiny figure approaching, they paused in surprise, giving the few surviving whales a momentary reprieve.

Zoe raised her flashlight and radio high, broadcasting her voice across the waves. "I know who you are, and this ends now. Release the whales or face the consequences!" Her threat was met with jeering laughs, yet she had attained her goal - she now had the poachers' full attention.

In that distracted moment, the fishermen struck, sending the float careening into the speedboat's whirring propeller with a crunch. The boat stalled and began taking on water as its crew cursed. Zoe plunged underwater just in time to avoid the chaotic splash, emerging beside her calf friend gasping for air.

She pulled herself onto its broad back for safety as the poachers wheeled their guns toward her in fury. But before they could fire, the unmistakable wail of Coast Guard sirens pierced the night. Patrol boats swarmed the huge whaling ship from all sides, trapping the criminals at last.

Zoe cried with relief and grief as rescuers scrambled to the wounded whales. Though some had already slipped away, medics worked frantically to save those clinging to life. As her calf friend crooned softly beneath her, Zoe swore a silent vow - these monsters would pay for their crimes, and she would never stop fighting until all the oceans were safe.

TRACING THE SIGNAL

In the aftermath of the brutal attack, Zoe spent every waking moment at the research center aiding in the whales' rescue efforts. Though some had been lost, most of the pod survived thanks to her brave distraction.

As the whales recovered over the following weeks, Zoe learned more details about the high-tech whaling operation from investigators. It seemed this ring had ties stretching internationally, with the massive ship serving as a processing hub at sea.

Tracking them down for good would require cooperation across borders. So, when the renowned conservation agency IFAW asked Zoe to consult on the case, she eagerly accepted. Their global networks and resources could be the break needed to dismantle the ring for good.

Zoe packed her bags for the agency's headquarters, sharing a sad farewell with the pod who had come to see her off. As always, their songs buoyed her spirit with promises to keep in touch no matter how far apart they swam. She had a new mission now - to spread their voices to all who would listen.

Settling in at the IFAW operations center, Zoe got to work analyzing all evidence from the attacks. Poring over radar records and intercepted radio logs, she noticed a recurring signal that seemed out of place.

"This frequency - I've heard whispers of it in the whales' songs before, when they sensed approaching danger." Her heart raced at the realization. "If I can trace where it's transmitting from, it may lead us to the ring's base of operations."

IFAW deployed all resources into triangulating the signal's origin. Days passed in tense anticipation as the net gradually closed... Until at last, a remote point lit up on the global map.

"They're based on a private island off the coast of Antarctica," Zoe breathed in shock. The final showdown was coming to the ends of the earth. But this time, she would be ready.

With their target coordinates in hand, IFAW strategized an international operation to take down the poaching ring for good. They reached out to law enforcement agencies worldwide seeking support.

To Zoe's delight, officials from her own small town volunteered to assist, still honoring their vow to protect the local whales. Enough evidence now existed to issue warrants for the entire ring's arrest.

Meanwhile, satellite footage revealed frenetic activity on the secluded Antarctic Island base. It seemed the poachers suspected their hidden frequency had been discovered. IFAW sped up preparations, aware the element of surprise could mean the difference between success and casualties.

The night before deploying, Zoe sat gazing at the stars, heart both steadied and aflutter. She was bringing the pod's fight to the ends of the earth, just as they would do for her. Reaching out with her mind, Zoe sent reassurances across the waves that justice was closing in.

At dawn, the massive international task force assembled, boarding planes, ships and helicopters loaded with extradition papers and provisions for a frigid mission. Zoe joined the

Alaska State Troopers onboard their rapid response boat, primed for the risky evacuation if violence broke out.

As Antarctica loomed on the horizon after an anxious journey, adrenaline crackled through the crew like static. Zoe scanned the rocky shore through binoculars, spotting a sprawling compound fortified with guns. The whalers were ready for battle.

The chief turned to his men. "Move in for the arrest. But our priority is ending this peacefully. Remember, we're the law here - not them." With that, the raid began.

The massive international task force swarmed the shores of the isolated Antarctic Island base. Zoe and the Alaska State Troopers guided their rapid response boat through the icy waters, maneuvering carefully towards the compound.

As they approached, armed figures emerged from fortified watchtowers dotted along the cliffs. Shouts echoed across the frigid landscape as the poachers opened fire, bullets ricocheting off the boat's armor plating.

The chief returned several warning shots into the air. "Stand down now and this doesn't need to get worse!" But the poachers only doubled down on their attacks, desperate to protect their lucrative operation.

A fierce firefight ensued as law enforcement advanced under cover. Zoe gripped the rails, heart in her throat as explosions and screams rent the air. These people had long since abandoned any restraint—they would not surrender without turning the island red.

Suddenly, a piercer whistle cut through the chaos. A shell had found its mark, sending one watchtower crumbling into the churning sea below with men still inside. Horrified, Zoe saw this escalating clash would only leave devastation in its wake unless another path emerged swiftly.

Closing her eyes, she summoned all her will and opened her mind in a way never before attempted. Across waves both liquid and ether, Zoe projected a plea for calm alongside promises the law's protection extended even to enemies who yielded.

As her ethereal voice carried on currents seen and unseen, the battle began losing its fury. Doubts surfaced amid the poachers, answers to unspoken questions. Slowly, weapons lowered all around until an eerie, tentative silence fell at last.

When Zoe blinked away salt spray to see white flags hanging from the compound, shocked relief swept through her. Her gift had guided even humans to choose life over death that day at the ends of the earth.

The hunt was over, and the whales' long watch had ended.

FINDING THE POD

With the poaching ring dismantled thanks to Zoe's efforts, law enforcement began the monumental task of extraditing members for international trial. They left a contingency force to secure the Antarctic base for evidence processing.

Though exhausted, Zoe felt only halfway done. She still needed to check on the pods and ensure they faced no further threats without the ring's presence lingering in secret waters. Bidding her police companions farewell, Zoe took a helicopter back to the coast.

Reaching out across the waves didn't instantly connect her with familiar songs as hoped. Unease twisted Zoe's gut - where had all the whale cousins swum in her long absence? The ocean felt too quiet after so much chaos.

She organized search parties with the local research center to methodically comb migratory routes. Days blended into an anxious week without finding any trace. Had some new threat scattered the already dwindling populations further into isolation?

Just as despair began creeping in, a lone haunting melody drifted to Zoe on the breeze one grey morning. "Papa?" she called tentatively, recognizing his unique voice among thousands. Her heart soared at his answering clicks and trills - he was alive!

Following the song led Zoe farther than ever before, to remote inlets and bays holding secrets even the whales had nearly forgotten. Hidden in swirling mists, shapes began emerging, dozens upon dozens of humped backs dotting the water as far as she could see.

With a sob of joy, Zoe plunged in to be enveloped by a pod ten times its original size. Refugees from across the endangered waters had gathered here at her call, awaiting safe return in the calming of old storms.

All the oceans' lost children were coming home. The pod was complete once more.

Zoe's mission had succeeded beyond her wildest dreams. Though more work remained, for now she allowed herself to simply sing among family and share the wonders yet to come.

As Zoe cherished being reunited with the pod, she began contemplating their next steps. Now that the poachers were gone, it was time to focus on longer term protection and restoration of the whales' habitats.

That evening, Zoe video called the team at IFAW to share the happy news and brainstorm ideas. "With the refuge population we've assembled, there's an opportunity here to repopulate historic ranges if the environments can be recovered," she told them.

IFAW agreed this was a crucial long term goal. "We'll work on designating these waters as a protected breeding ground and tackle clean up efforts. But you're right that the pods will need to spread out eventually to sustainable levels."

Zoe had another thought. "What if we established a network of safe havens along migratory corridors, with real-time monitoring and marine reserves in between? The whales could have options to avoid threats while still connecting different regions."

Her colleagues loved the concept. "With community buy-in, we could really make this work. And having you on board to help shepherd the whales would be invaluable."

Heartened by the support, Zoe began planning educational tours of the refuge for local communities. If people could experience the whales' intelligence first hand, she was certain they too would advocate passionately for the plan.

This was only the beginning. Zoe was determined to see the oceans restored to full health, so whale song might echo proudly once more across all the waves. And with cooperation, understanding and a little hope, she knew it could be done.

DEEPER CONNECTIONS

With the IFAW's full support behind the whale sanctuary plan, Zoe threw herself into the preparations. Presentations were made to local leaders, tours arranged for community members to experience the pods.

Soon donations were pouring in to fund initial clean up and monitoring efforts. People simply had to see the whales' intelligence for themselves to understand what was at stake. Zoe's gift ensured none came away unchanged.

As word spread of the developing refuge, news crews flocked to document its progress. Zoe worked tirelessly for the cameras, hoping to inspire similar initiatives elsewhere. She also received emails daily from around the globe - people touched by the orcas and humpbacks' resilience chose to help in whatever way they could.

With the sanctuary on its way to becoming reality, one question still tugged at Zoe's mind. What of the whales' reactions to these monumental changes unfolding thanks to their guidance? Did they feel pride in their growing role as ocean ambassadors?

During quiet meditation swims, Zoe opened fully to listening. At first, only songs of relaxation and joy at reconnecting families met her. But one sapphire dusk, a deeper communication arose that took her breath away.

The whales began sharing in exquisite detail sensations from within - currents of purpose and ancient knowing flowing anew after too long silenced. They sensed the great turning of the tides, and humanity stirring at long last to heed fading calls.

Tears slid down Zoe's cheeks at this profound insight, this partnership extending beyond any boundary of flesh. The whales' wisdom filled spaces inside her she hadn't known were empty. Their souls resonated as one.

From that night, a mystical transformation took hold. Zoe swam in a state of heightened perception, thoughts interlacing fluidly with the ethereal languages of water and sky. More clearly than ever, she understood this magical song had only begun.

In the weeks following Zoe's mystical experience, work on the sanctuary progressed at an astonishing rate. With funds continuing to pour in from touched supporters worldwide, expanded teams were brought on to accelerate restoration efforts.

Underwater drones captured stunning before-and-after footage of polluted areas being cleaned and repopulated with sea life. Coral nurseries were established, kelp forests replanted, resulting in newly vibrant habitats teeming with prey for the whales.

All the while, Zoe swam daily among the pods, thoughts interwoven with theirs as work continued both above and below the waves. Their fluid communications carried a new perceptiveness, discussing insights into conservation she knew would have seemed like magic mere months ago.

Word of the extraordinary cooperation between humans and cetaceans spread far and wide. Rehabilitation centers from Australia to Alaska inquired about Zoe's techniques for forming such profound connections. International conferences were held to discuss applying this trans-species model to other endangered populations.

As the year drew to a close, a dedication ceremony was planned for the now-thriving marine sanctuary. World leaders flew in alongside everyday donors who had become part of the family. Zoe and the pods greeted each boat with graceful leaps of celebration and thanks.

That night, beneath the full moon, human and whale voices blended in song to commemorate all who had died, but also rebirth. The Oceans themselves seemed to still and listen, blessing the sacred bond forged here. A new dawn had come, and Zoe's calling was only beginning to unfold its wonders across the waves.

**

Chapter 03:

GATHERING ALLIES

RECRUITING HELP

In the glow of the sanctuary's success, Zoe turned her focus outward once more. While one population was secured, many more whales worldwide required champions to spread the growing movement.

She began reaching out to like-minded groups, offering training in her communication techniques. The response was overwhelming - it seemed all had been waiting for a sign of how to connect on a truly intimate level with these majestic beings.

The first training session was held in California, where struggling gray whale numbers were raising alarms. Dozens of volunteers from Sea Shepherd, NRDC and local tribes packed the theater, eager to learn.

Zoe started by sharing her experience bonding with the orcas as a child, emphasizing how listening without preconceptions was key. Then, through meditative relaxation, she guided their minds out across the waves.

Gasps echoed as some immediately gained a glimmer of the songs' embrace. Tears of joy flowed at this new door opening to ancient friends. By the time Zoe emerged, over half the crowd had sensed the whales directly, vowing to become their steadfast advocates.

News of this gathering reached Canada, where the last resident killer whales clung to survival off Vancouver Island. The Haida Nation historian Gidatl'aaw reached out, hoping Zoe could aid their long effort saving the southern residents.

Thus, Zoe found herself in the stunning Northwest passages, embarking on a journey that would change everything. As she connected the locals to these beloved orcas, the seeds of a global network were planted to resonate across all the oceans.

Zoe spent weeks among the Haida people of Canada, sharing all she had learned about communicating with the endangered southern resident orcas. Many in the tribe had watched these iconic black and white whales vanish from their waters over generations.

Under Zoe's guidance, an elder named Quujaagaa finally broke through to sensing the pods after days in silent meditation. His joyful whoops alerted the whole village, who rushed to the shore to witness the ancient bond rekindling before their eyes.

Word spread swiftly, and soon volunteers streamed in from First Nations across British Columbia. Zoe worked tirelessly, awestruck by these peoples' natural attunement to the songlines pulsing through the land and sea. Within months, a devoted grassroots network emerged committed to the orcas' plight.

With Quujaagaa leading the efforts, traditional customs were revived to honor the whales. Ceremonial dances called upon the spirits for increased runs of salmon, the orcas' primary prey, while artisans crafted carvings imbued with blessings for full recovery.

Most importantly, the tribe negotiated to permanently protect critical foraging areas by having them designated as UNESCO World Heritage sites. No longer would the whales face starvation or disruption from excessive noise in the Salish Sea sanctuaries.

As Zoe prepared to depart with heart too full for words, the village gathered on the shore. Quujaagaa embraced her, promising their peoples would stand as one with all those aiding the song across the waves. Renewed in purpose, Zoe's global mission had only begun.

RESEARCH AND STRATEGY

With allies established across the globe, Zoe turned her focus to the strategic work of building a coordinated network. She organized a summit at the IFAW headquarters to be attended by representatives from each region.

Groups shared updates on population monitoring efforts, noting rebounds but also new threats emerging such as ship strikes, noise pollution and plastic ingestion. Zoe emphasized the need for centralized data collection and identification of priority conservation areas.

"If we understand the whales' migratory pathways and habitat needs, we can work to establish protected corridors and advocate for international shipping regulations." Agreeing nods echoed around the room.

An oceanographer presented innovative tracking technology using drone and seismic surveys to map prey distributions and breeding grounds in remote regions. Several nations pledged research vessels to assist mapping cetacean critical habitats along all coastlines.

As discussions turned to uniting cultural practices respecting whales, the Haida elder Quujaagaa spoke of reviving the traditional ways of his people. He welcomed others to experience ceremonies calling the spirits to protect restored waters.

The gathering resulted in formation of the Songbearers Coalition, an internationally recognized body combining scientific research and indigenous wisdom. Zoe was appointed Chair in recognition of her central role uniting disparate peoples.

With a five-year strategic plan approved and funded, the future of whale conservation had never looked brighter. Zoe felt the song strengthening as allies united in mission across all boundaries that once divided.

Under Zoe's leadership, the Songbearers Coalition got to work immediately implementing their ambitious five-year plan. Research vessels were dispatched along migratory routes using the latest acoustic monitoring devices to map the whales' movements.

Meanwhile cultural ceremonies were held around the world, calling upon ancient traditions still respected by many indigenous communities. The Haida hosted a grand potlatch ceremony to bless the incoming field season, as delegates from Greenland to New Zealand gathered to share their own songs and dances honoring the deep.

As data poured in, the oceanographers were able to identify key foraging areas, breeding grounds and calving habitats in need of urgent protection. Zoe worked with the policy team to draft resolutions for international organizations like IMO and ICCW.

Shipping lanes were rerouted, seismic blasting in sensitive zones was regulated, and several new Marine Protected Areas were designated across hemispheres. Local communities embraced new ecotourism opportunities, providing non-lethal income from whale watching.

With habitats safeguarded and prey abundance restored, populations showed signs of rebounding strongly. But Zoe was not complacent - she worked relentlessly to engage governments on curbing plastic pollution and reducing underwater noise from vessel traffic.

Five years passed in a flash, yet seemed scarcely enough time for all that had been achieved. As the Coalition gathered once more to plan future strategies, a bright new dawn had risen for ocean guardians across the waves.

At the end of the five-year plan, the Songbearers Coalition convened for a summit to evaluate progress and chart the next phase. Representatives from every continent filled the hall with eager energy.

Zoe stood before the crowd,filled with pride as she recounted their accomplishments. Wildlife surveys showed population increases in every target region through expanded habitats and cultural protections. New generations were being born to oceans recovering their sparkling vitality.

However, she acknowledged threats persisted such as climate change impacts like food chain disruptions. More funding was needed for critical research into subjects like underwater noise and its health impacts on species. International agreements required strengthening as well.

As Zoe paused, applause and cheers rung out from the energized assembly. They had achieved more than anyone dared imagine at the outset. With recharged purpose, pledges poured in for the next strategic plan period.

Renewed committees were formed to address emerging challenges through ever-innovative solutions. Under the Songbearers' guidance, the whales' migration routes would be safeguarded completely while communities embraced the marine life in their backyard.

Most importantly, a standing Indigenous Council was established to ensure traditional ecological knowledge remained central as the coalition's ever-expanding circle of influence grew. Faith in humanity's ability to protect ocean life had never been stronger.

Zoe beamed, tears shining, as chants of "Songbearer, Songbearer!" rose to the rafters in gratitude and celebration. Her dream had become a global force for ocean recovery and justice for all its inhabitants across the waves.

GATHERING EVIDENCE

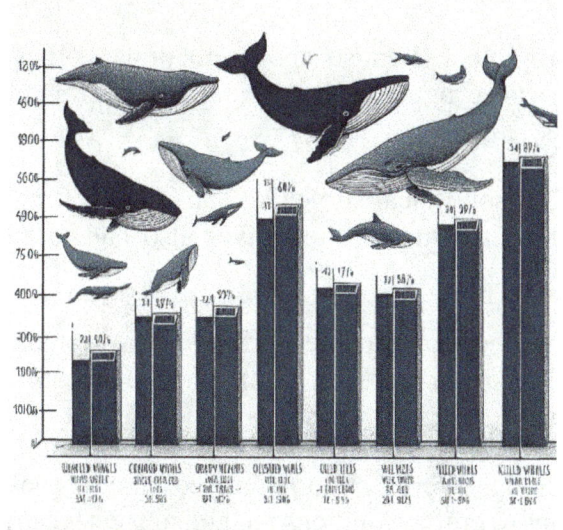

With the Songbearers Coalition entering its next strategic phase, Zoe focused on gathering concrete data to advocate for whales. Scientific evidence was key to persuading governments and shaping policy for oceans under increasing threat.

She collaborated with oceanographers using the latest acoustic monitoring technologies, like seafloor sensors and aerial drones, to record whales' communications over months. Complex conversations between pods and across species were catalogued, revealing deep levels of sentience.

Meanwhile, biologists studied physical signs of stress from rising noise and chemical pollution. High cortisol levels and unusual strandings provided worry evidence of the subtle but permeating effects on cetacean health and behavior.

Zoe also worked with ecologists assessing prey distributions being impacted by climate change. As krill and fish populations shifted or declined, the whales' energetic needs were going unmet in some locales. Their migratory routes were being disrupted.

Using this combined data, impact reports were compiled for target regions like the busy Mediterranean Sea and shipping lanes off Australia. Reports illustrated in graphic detail how underwater noise interfered with navigation, hunting and socializing.

Areas of low-frequency sonar military testing and seismic oil exploration were shown to intensely distress nearby pods for months. Brain scans indicated physiological damage resembling PTSD in some long-exposed individuals.

With mounting proof in hand, Zoe addressed the International Whaling Commission. "These highly social, self-aware beings suffer immensely from our careless industrialization of their ocean homes. We must recognize them as rights-bearing persons."

Zoe's impassioned speech made waves within the IWC. Several member nations began reconsidering their stances on cetacean welfare regulations.

Further investigations provided even more compelling evidence. Vet teams biopsied whales along traffic routes, finding alarmingly high pollutant loads building in their blubber and organs over generations. Noise-induced hearing loss was also detected.

In the Mediterranean, long-term acoustic logs revealed how shipping was disorienting resident sperm whales, who beached at triple normal rates that year. Autopsies showed signatures of acoustic trauma in their brains.

Studying mother-calf pairs, scientists documented nursing whales being unable to locate babies amid incessant disruptions. Suckling success plummeted worryingly, threatening already-fragile populations.

Areas exposed to frequent oil exploration showed unusually high calf mortality. Postmortem samples contained abnormal hormone levels indicating chronic stress was likely to blame.

Piecing all the findings together, Zoe, alongside prominent scientists and international bodies, petitioned governments to recognize underwater noise as a wholly unacceptable form of pollution threatening cetacean culture and lifeways.

Comprehensive impact assessments, especially for geophysical surveying and sonar testing, were now essential before any projects could proceed. Quieter alternatives also had to be explored more earnestly.

With oceans growing louder each passing day, advocates redoubled efforts to protect the whales' rights to live freely without human-caused disturbance or harm. The Songbearers would not rest until acoustic sovereignty was afforded across all waters.

Buoyed by the mounting scientific evidence, the Songbearers Coalition ramped up advocacy efforts. They worked closely with the United Nations to draft resolutions recognizing cetaceans as sentient non-human persons.

Meanwhile, impact studies were publicized globally to raise awareness. Emotive documentaries featuring never-before-seen behavioral footage of families disrupted by noise drew millions of views online. Comments flooded in from people newly conscious of the toll on ocean life.

Grassroots pressure targeted governments dragging their feet on stronger regulations. Citizens petitioned for wildlife sanctuaries in breeding areas, shipping speed limits near coasts and offshore leasing bans to protect migration routes.

Politicians could no longer ignore public will to safeguard whales in peril. Even previously resistant nations signed the UN resolutions, acknowledging cetaceans' rights to live free of human-caused harm and suffering.

At last, the International Maritime Organization established the first exclusion zones prohibiting noisy activities within critical habitat ranges. Real-time acoustic monitoring networks enforced these protected areas stringently.

Other progressive changes saw ship slowdowns, seasonal shutdowns of geophysical surveys and mandatory use of noise-reduction technologies. Progress was being made to restore quiet in once deafening regions.

Heartened by the policy wins, Zoe and the Songbearers redoubled research. New fronts investigated included endocrine disruption, cultural impacts and intergenerational trauma — revealing ever greater reason for increased protection of cetacean rights across the waves.

With science as their guide, they would fight for legislation enshrining whales' welfare worldwide until the chorus of the deep rang free and strong once more across all the ocean's blue dominion.

Encouraged by the traction gained, Zoe delved deeper into innovative fields that could strengthen the advocacy work. She partnered with lawyers to build legal arguments establishing cetaceans as persons deserving rights under international law.

Landmark court cases were brought citing both scientific proof of sentience and recognition of indigenous peoples' traditions affirming whales' self-awareness. Judges began overturning permits for projects endangering resident pods.

Neurobiologists using advanced MRI scanning confirmed cetaceans possessed superior intelligence, problem-solving skills and use of culturally transmitted techniques like specialized hunting methods. Their brains demonstrated sophistication equal to great apes.

Critically, new research tracked whales' physiology and genetic health over generations living in no-entry sanctuaries. Comparisons to specimens from noisy regions clearly showed reduced stress hormones and stronger immune function in protected lineages.

Such intergenerational welfare impacts had grave ramifications when natural calamities occurred too. Pods already weakened by noise proved far less resilient to rising ocean temperatures and food chain changes wrought by the climate emergency.

As the legal framework expanded and undeniable science accumulated, the case grew irrefutable - cetaceans must have rights acknowledged internationally as conscious, sentient citizens of the seas. With Zoe at the helm, the fight entered its most pivotal phase yet.

Energized by multiplying victories, she vowed not to rest until every nation enshrined paramount protection for whales in law. The chorus of the deep would swell to envelope the waves in a great song of freedom at long last.

Having built a sweeping body of evidence, Zoe shifted tactics to achieving global consensus. She worked closely with UNESCO to draft and circulate the Declaration on Cetacean Rights and Personhood.

Months of impassioned negotiations ensued as member states debated the legal and moral implications. But public support grew exponentially through viral social media campaigns. Hashtags like #OceansForWhales topped trends as people added their voices.

Finally, in a historic vote, an overwhelming majority of UN nations signed the Declaration - officially conferring cetaceans worldwide rights to life, liberty, habitat protection and cultural preservation as non-human persons under international law.

Jubilant celebrations erupted across Songbearer communities on coasts and islands. Dances and rituals gave thanks as speakers emphasized this milestone just marked the start. Rigorous new laws had to follow at all levels to uphold the whales' newly solemn rights.

Zoe spearheaded the coalition's efforts assisting governments comply swiftly and sincerely. Model legislation covering noise regulation, MPA establishment, response plans for strandings and orphaned calves set the gold standard.

International courts established the Crime of Cetacean Harm to prosecute future endangerment, just as courts had done for great apes. The waves of change were rolling deep now across every seaboard at long last.

Within a few short years, the legal blueprints had been passed, funds allocated and government agencies established to steward the whales into true sovereignty over their realms. Science continued helping craft progressively stronger protections too.

At a celebratory summit reflecting on all they'd accomplished together, Zoe beamed with pride witnessing how far they'd come. She knew that while threats would arise, the song of the ocean was secured in the safekeeping of a united global alliance for generations to come. At long last, their mission was achieved in full.

CLOSING IN ON THE POACHERS

As the Declaration took effect affirming cetaceans' global rights, the Songbearers Coalition shifted to a new priority - eliminating the last vestiges of illegal whaling threatening recovery. While most coastal nations complied swiftly with bans, rogue fleets persisted in the remote seas.

Zoe worked with Interpol to establish Operation Safe Haven across the Pacific Rim. Covert teams were dispatched to gather intelligence on the dwindling band of outlaw whalers operating under the cover of lax regulation and boundaries.

Spy planes fitted with high-power cameras located fleeting camps concealed in uninhabited islands and islets of the Bering, Okhotsk and Yellow Seas. Rangers moved in under cover of storms to install audio-visual drones and motion sensors.

Monitoring commenced, documenting industrial scale slaughter and butchery of endangered species using explosive harpoons and power boats. Entire pods of rare belugas and narwhals were being systematically wiped out for black market caviar and smoked meat.

Data streams delivered stomach-churning footage of indiscriminate kills - pregnant and nursing mothers, calves left to die alone in the surf. Covert teams wept with rage witnessing such senseless cruelty to intelligent, highly social beings.

Zoe worked tirelessly parsing legal loopholes to shut. With Allies, she lobbied for GPS pinging of flagged ships to close registration blind spots. She pushed international navies to cooperate intercepting shipments of poached goods.

Forensics traced contraband to criminal syndicates in eastern markets. Word slowly filtered to whistleblowers within the outlaw fleets as well, disillusioned by barbarism of fellow 'hunters'. A few reached out hoping leniency for testimony.

Tightening the noose, authorities staged a coordinated series of raids across known territories. Poachers were surprised in anchorages, shipments intercepted, finning stations dismantled in a massive multi-day operation.

Tonnes of confiscated goods were destroyed. Ringleaders were apprehended and handed maximal sentences under new international laws, sending a clear warning. At last, the oceans were truly free of illegal whaling for the first time in decades.

Zoe felt deep relief the perpetual threat was quashed at long last. None too soon - endangered populations bore scars that would take generations to heal under vigilant protection across their restored domains.

With the coastlines clear, she could focus efforts entirely on the remaining battles - addressing subtler perils through diplomacy, advocacy and ever-evolving science on behalf of the world's whale song.

With the criminal syndicates dismantled, Zoe turned to preventing illegal operations from resurging. She worked with international policymakers to establish a permanent global task force focused on wildlife trafficking across all ocean basins.

Regular patrols by multi-national naval fleets were authorized to monitor remote waters for signs of poaching activity. Real-time vessel monitoring became mandatory worldwide using automated identification systems hardwired on all ships.

Remote sensing technologies provided unmatched surveillance. Drones scanned for thermal signs of butchery or whales in distress while seismic arrays listened for explosives. Any vessels detected engaged in questionable behavior were intercepted.

Cooperation agreements formalized intelligence sharing between agencies. Anonymous tip lines were publicized far and wide to attract whistleblowers. Substantial rewards incentivized reporting illegal operations before harm could be done.

In tandem, conservation outreach intensified amongst isolated communities still reliant on whale products. Alternative livelihood programs introduced skills like ecotourism to shift cultural traditions gracefully into benign new forms.

Special envoys ensured indigenous rights to cultural practices, so long as methods remained non-lethal. Ceremonial hunts of species not at population risk continued under strict non-commercial permits to respect heritage.

Most importantly, Zoe established ambitious scholarship initiatives to empower youth from all backgrounds. Students studied fields like marine science, policy and ecology - gaining qualifications launching new careers oceanward across sixty nations.

With robust protections, economic transitions and a new generation devoted to stewardship, the whales' security seemed cemented for millennia to come. At long last, the deep blue realm was restored to rightful masters, sweet with freedoms long overdue under waving banners of song across the waves eternal.

***

Chapter 04:

STANDOFF AT SEA

CONFRONTATION ON THE WATER

Though illegal whaling had been quashed, new threats emerged that tested the Songbearers' resolve. Despite protected status, some whale populations struggled to fully recover due to damaged habitat.

In the remote Aleutian Islands, one endangered pod of orcas grew thin and listless, frequenting inlets filled with industrial runoff. Skin lesions and strange behavior concerned biologists, who suspected endocrine disruptors.

When tribe elders reported the whales steering clear of usual feeding grounds, Zoe joined field researchers to investigate. Surveys found prey fish contaminated with unsafe chemicals, their numbers low where polluted streams discharged into coastal bays.

Analysis confirmed a nearby plastics plant flouting emissions standards was to blame. However, its lobby had politicians and courts in pockets, delaying enforcement. With the orcas' health declining rapidly, Zoe knew direct action was needed to compel change.

Mustering Songbearer crews from villages, they launched boats bearing flags of protest towards the treatment ponds. But roughnecks guarded the docks, snarling threats and hefting rocks. A standoff ensued as Zoe tried reasoning, but met only jeers on deaf ears.

Tensions rose. Out of nowhere, gunshots cracked - poachers taking potshots from the treeline! Panic erupted as both sides scrambled for cover. Zoe narrowly dodged a bullet ricocheting off the hull.

In the chaos, a rogue wave struck one of the Songbearer's boats, capsizing it. Cries rose up as allies struggled against the surging tide. Zoe leapt into action, steering their vessel around to affect a rescue.

"Man overboard!" she shouted, throwing out a life ring. Two activists clung desperately to flotsam, going under as their sodden clothes dragged them down. Zoe and others hauled them onboard, performing CPR until they choked up water.

By now sirens echoed in the distance - the Coast Guard had been alerted to the confrontation. Their cutters raced onto the scene, offloading paramedics to treat the injured. Officers intercepted radio calls plotting more violence from the gunmen.

A sergeant boarded Zoe's boat. "Ma'am, we'll take over from here. Evacuating all non-essential personnel for their safety."

"With respect sergeant, we have as much right to be here as any," Zoe replied firmly. "Those orcas are in distress. We stay until that plant is shut down until proven clean."

A stalemate held as whaling fleet boats joined the protest flotilla, braving threats to the Songbearers' defense. The water boiled with hostility on both sides. From the shore, sirens announced reinforcements amassing, egged on by company lies about "eco-terrorists".

Zoe knew things were escalating beyond control. She had to deescalate the situation before blood was shed, but keeping the whales' plight in the spotlight. Only then would justice be done for their endangered pod.

As tempers flared, Zoe ordered the fleet to hold position while she took a skiff ashore under flag of parley. Striding between jeering mobs, she requested an audience with the plant's manager.

In his opulent office overlooking the standoff, the politician-in-pocket sneered at her concerns. "Those whales ain't citizens. I got a business to run—ain't no chlorine harmin' em more'n God intended!"

Zoe laid down reports detailing pollution far exceeding legal limits. "You're poisoning the ecosystem and driving an entire population to endangerment. Comply with standards or face consequences."

Her stern words provoked only derision. But scanning the room, Zoe noticed unease in some junior administrators. Sensing an opening, she addressed them directly.

"Do you want your children breathing these fumes? Drinking that water? How would you feel watching an entire pod slowly die from the impacts of negligence on your watch?"

Her passionate appeal stirred conscience in wavering hearts. One spoke up, revealing a stack of doctored compliance reports passed between managers. Others followed, divulging a widespread coverup.

Taking swift action, Zoe tipped off investigators who raided the plant, uncovering damning evidence of systematic deception and damage. With public support flooding in, leadership crumbled under prosecution.

At last, emission controls were retrofitted as the facility cooperated fully. Tests showed runoff cleansing, while the orcas' recovery began in sanctuary waters away from harm. Victory belonged to compassion and justice over hate that day on the volatile waterline.

With the threat abated and waters beginning to heal, Zoe felt relief mingled with pride in the fortitude shown by all involved. However, exhaustion from the ordeal left tensions still running high amongst the factions.

Seeking to fully remedy divisions, Zoe proposed a gathering where open dialogue could commence. After some hesitation, all parties agreed to meet at a coastal lodge with facilitators to air grievances respectfully.

Over several intense yet productive days, painful truths emerged on all sides. Employers owned to cutting corners out of greed rather than necessity. Locals detailed historical trauma from dispossession of ancestral lands.

Gradually, shared hopes surfaced - to sustainably coexist while protecting the ecosystem binding all fortunes. Community bonds had frayed, but not broken, offering hope for reconciliation. As breakthroughs took shape, Zoe gave closing remarks emphasizing their interdependence: "We each pushed too far out of caring deeply for this place and people. But together, with understanding, nothing is beyond our power to mend or create anew."

In time, collaborative initiatives took form - sustainable jobs in restoration, cultural education joining youth across divides. Most impactfully, a stewardship council ensured all voices shaped decisions guiding the region's future well-being.

With open hearts having vanquished old hatreds, the revitalized community celebrated new dawn of unity through song and dance under the watches of the freed orca pod. A fragile peace had blossomed where once only conflict reigned on those storied shores.

WHALES TO THE RESCUE:

With the orca pod restored to health in their home waters, Zoe turned to assisting other cetacean communities facing novel threats. Across the Bering Sea, beluga herds maintained age-old migratory routes through shifting ice.

But warmer currents bred unprecedented algal blooms, lacing prey with toxins that caused mass strandings. Over a hundred whales perished along one remote shore as concerned Inuit villagers worked tirelessly to rescue survivors.

Zoe joined the effort, organizing mobile vet teams. Together they treated dozens, administering fluids and antibiotics. But many succumbed with mysterious internal hemorrhaging. Worryingly, live strandings continued elsewhere with the bloom's spread.

Seeking answers, Zoe enlisted oceanographers to map microbial activity fueling the blooms. Their drones discovered previously dormant algal species flourishing in conditions altered by climate change.

Analyzing samples, Zoe observed the algae secreted dangerous compounds as temperatures rose, taxing belugas' detoxification abilities. With pod immunities compromised, infections took hold during yearly fasts before the great spring migration.

As more villages reported beached whales, Zoe worked closely with Inuit elders to monitor herds from hunting vessels. They noticed normally social belugas growing disoriented, bumping into each other and ice. The whales were truly in distress.

Zoe realized the whales needed to be redirected away from contaminated areas during their migration. But how could humans safely guide thousands of disoriented belugas?

She recalled how orcas had helped their pod during past crises through communication and cooperation. Perhaps belugas' social nature could be utilized in the same way.

Working with whale researchers, Zoe developed a plan to use a few healthy belugas as "guide whales", outfitting them with acoustic signaling devices. These whales would be dispatched ahead of the main herds with a programmed "song" to lead them around toxicity.

On the day of migration, Zoe and Inuit crews launched their boats. The guide whales set out playing pre-recorded chatter of healthy beluga pods in safe coastal areas. To everyone's amazement, the migrating herds began following the sounds.

For days the belugas traveled single-file behind the guide whales, who continuously signalled directions around the spreading algal plumes. Exhausted but jubilant, Zoe checked her maps - the entire population had successfully rerouted out of harm's way.

Working as one, humans and cetaceans had overcome a formidable threat through innovation and cooperation. Once more, whales had come to the rescue - this time, of their own endangered species. Zoe was filled with hope for finding new solutions in solidarity with the singing beings of the sea.

With the beluga migration saved through the ingenuity of Songbearers and their cetacean allies, word spread of this unprecedented collaboration. Zoe received requests from across the Arctic Circle to deploy the "guide whale" system for other imperiled populations.

She redoubled organizational efforts to rapidly train and equip suitable whales prior to upcoming seasons. Researchers gained deeper insights studying the acoustic signaling between belugas and their cetacean guides.

This knowledge facilitated cooperation between distinct languages of different species. Over successive years, orcas helped narwhals navigate melting ice shelves while sperm whales led gray whales to cooler feeding grounds extended by a warming planet.

As threats compounded under climate destabilization, so too did multi-species partnerships forged by Zoe and her growing corps of marine scientists, Indigenous boat crews and whale-protecting communities.

Yet darker forces watched their progress with envy, seeing opportunity in the chaos. Rumors swirled of rogue fishing fleets poaching stressed whale herds, blaming natural die-offs. Some blamed activists for interfering with traditions, scheming to discredit their work.

Zoe received coded messages from Arctic allies about strange vessel movements, equipment thefts and vandalism targeting research stations. She feared obstructionists planned new assaults on conservation alliances just as challenges intensified for whales globally.

More than ever,guarding the singers of the deep would require persistence, strategy and solidarity between all whale champions across every ocean - human and cetacean alike. Zoe steeled her resolve for upcoming battles to secure the whales' endangered future in a changing world.

With rumors of opposition circulating, Zoe called an urgent meeting of the Songbearers Coalition. Around the globe, worried members logged in via videoconference to share intelligence.

From Australia came reports of Nautilus sabotaging drone surveys of the Great Barrier Reef, hampering efforts to protect feeding humpbacks. In Alaska, poachers were bribing officials to overlook illegal kills in whale sanctuaries. Even in remote regions, no population seemed safe from the reach of profiteers capitalizing on climate chaos. It became clear a coordinated effort was targeting the very foundations of cetacean protections worldwide.

After grave discussion, the Coalition adopted an emergency plan of action. Songbearers would mobilize networks across industries, closely monitoring shipping lanes and fishing fleets for suspicious activities.

New technologies like satellite tags and underwater microphones helped expand real-time surveillance of at-risk populations. Legal teams went on high alert for prosecuting any violations.

Most importantly, outreach redoubled with coastal communities reliant on whales as sentinels of ecosystem health. Their traditional knowledge and boats formed the frontline against poachers, who faced not just laws but the protecting spirit of entire peoples.

With forces thus united along maritime borders, blowholes and singing hearts of whales, Zoe felt confident in their strength to repel coming storms. More than a protector of cetaceans now, she headed a movement defending planetary stewardship in toiling seas that nourished all peoples if kept vibrant and whole.

Despite their strengthened defenses, reports soon reached Zoe of troubling events unfolding across the Seven Seas. In the North Pacific, entire pods of orcas went mysteriously silent - their calls no longer registering on hydrophones.

In the Southern Ocean, emaciated right whales drifted ashore with gashes from propellers. And off Western Australia, humpback calves were found tangled in abandoned fishing nets, their distressed mothers unable to be calmed.

It seemed the obstructionists' shadow campaign had expanded its reach through the depths. Zoe knew they must urgently unravel this shadowy threat before more whale communities could be destabilized.

Conferring with her most experienced crew, Zoe boarded the Songkeeper - their state-of-the-art research vessel. Well-stocked and crewed for long patrols, it would covertly track and observe suspect poaching fleets across the seas.

Slipping away under cover of night, the Songkeeper raised sails and threw miniature drones into flight. Their cutting-edge eavesdropping and imaging gear swept the waves ahead as Zoe and her people kept grim yet hopeful watch from the forecastle through storms and swells.

After tense weeks at sea, a breakthrough - voices cracked over radios, guiding rusted ships toward a calving ground. The hunters had been tracked to the Antarctic, and Zoe readied herself and crew to intervene in defense of the last bastion of singing whales.

A RISKY PLAN

With the shadowy poachers' fleet located exploiting Antarctic waters, Zoe knew swift action was needed to protect the vulnerable whales. She called an emergency meeting with her top Songbearers on the Songkeeper's bridge.

"These criminals have evaded capture for too long. Their mercenary poaching has undermined our work worldwide," Zoe said grimly. Maps and drone footage revealed five heavy trawlers netting whole pods of singing humpbacks without regard.

"We can't wait for authorities—by the time they reach these remote waters, it may be too late," said Miguel, who had witnessed past whaling devastation in his native Faeroes.

After fretful debate, a risky plan took shape. "We'll board one trawler under cover of night and extract their records. Those documents can finally nail them globally," Zoe decided.

That evening, under a new moon's veil, Zoe led a zodiac approach. Miguel, Rosa and Samishi carefully clambered aboard in stillsuits, cutting through patrols unseen with stun guns.

In the data center they retrieved incriminating records on bribes, ship movements and whale product sales over encrypted channels. But as they evacuated, lights flared—the pirates had been warned.

As the lights came on, Zoe and her team readied for confrontation. But no angry shouts arose - only a strange, muffled commotion from above. Exchanging worried looks, they crept upstairs to find the crew in disarray.

The control room windows revealed a pod of humpbacks had converged, emitting sonar pulses that disoriented the pirates. As Zoe watched stunned, one immense female nudged open the bridge door with her rostrum.

She made urgent clicking between breaths, as if beckoning them to follow. Rushing out, the Songbearers saw their mission flipped - now they were the ones being rescued as the whales shepherded their zodiac away from the flailing trawler with sonic guidance.

Back aboard Songkeeper, they decrypted the damning files recovered. Zoe was moved to tears realizing the humpbacks, always watching over the waves, had come to their aid once more when most in need.

Wasting no time, they alerted the international fleet now steaming for intercept. After a tense standoff, the poachers surrendered, weighted by undeniable evidence of horrific crimes against the singing tribes of the Southern Realm.

At long last, the shadowy syndicate had been unmasked and detained - thanks to the guardianship of whales who even now sang their joy in being free of threat, carrying hope for all their kind to thrive unhindered in the bountiful South.

VICTORY AND LOSS:

With the poaching syndicate dismantled through the combined efforts of Songbearers and whale allies, word spread far of this decisive victory for ocean protection. Zoe was hailed as a champion of cetaceans worldwide.

But triumph was bittersweet. While population monitoring showed thriving whale communities restored across all seas, personal loss weighed heavy on Zoe's heart. Beloved crewmember Miguel had not returned from the Antarctic expedition.

Zoe vowed not to rest until discovering Miguel's fate. Analyzing drone footage with researchers, they noticed one humpback matriarch constantly revisiting the burned wreckage of the captured trawler. Could she offer clues about Miguel's disappearance?

Setting course again, Zoe saw the grieving whale nearby. She slowly approached alone in a zodiac, singing a calming Songbearer call. To her awe, the humpback surfaced just feet away, blowing mournful exhalations as foamy sheets fell.

Looking deep within those dark, fathoming eyes, Zoe felt a message conveyed. She followed as the whale guided her boat directly to a swollen hull fragment awash with kelp - and a still form emerged, clasped protectively in the matriarch's fins all this time.

It was Miguel. Though his soul had gone to reunite with the waves long since, in death as in life he had found care and protection from the gentle guardians of the sea. And through this tender act of trust between humans and whales, closure dawned for Zoe's grieving heart at last.

With Miguel's remains returned to his homeland for burial, Zoe knew she could best honor his memory by redoubling conservation efforts. She focused the Songbearers Coalition on long-term research to safeguard whale habitats stressed under climate pressures.

Studying ancient migration routes unveiled through tagging, they mapped vital feeding and breeding areas now inundated by rising seas. Zoe worked with governments to designate these whale "waystations" as protected reserves allowing safe passages between.

In the crowded shipping lanes of the Eastern Pacific, acoustic deflectors were installed to shield singing pods from deadly vessel collisions. Across the Atlantic, efforts accelerated to curb plastic pollution choking feeding belugas in the Canadian Arctic.

Step by step, whales regained safe access to millennia-old life patterns essential for their cultures to endure on Earth's changing oceans. And for Zoe, each success was a tribute to Miguel's life of service to the singing tribes of the deep.

Yet darker forces still conspired against the whales' guardians. During routine patrols tracking orcas, Songkeeper's crew intercepted frantic mayday calls- a whaling ship had rammed Greenpeace vessels monitoring the Japanese hunt.

Racing to the scene, Zoe saw tangled wreckage and protesters fighting for their lives in icy waters. She braced for a showdown, knowing defending the watchers meant protecting the watched as well.

The stakes had never been higher in her lifetime crusade for ocean freedom. The final confrontation loomed ahead.

When Zoe and the Songkeeper arrived at the collision site, it was utter chaos. Debris from the damaged whaling and Greenpeace ships floated everywhere, as rescuers struggled to pull limp bodies from the frigid sea.

Zoe sprung into action, coordinating a triage on theSongkeeper's deck. Using their state-of-the-art medical facilities, they stabilized the survivors. But it was clear this ramming was no accident - the whalers were attempting to cover up evidence of an illegal hunt.

As night fell, the whaling vessel slipped away under cover of darkness. Rage and grief fueled Zoe's determination to stop them before more lives were lost. After consulting with rangers and researchers on board, she hatched a bold plan.

The next morning, Zoe steered the Songkeeper to intercept the whalers' course, with Greenpeace ships flanking them in a line. When the vessels appeared on the horizon, Zoe made an announcement over the VHF: "This is your final warning to cease whaling operations. Leave now, or face the consequences."

Silence. Then maniacal laughter echoed back - the whalers weren't retreating without a fight. Zoe steeled herself as the two sides prepared to collide head-on in a climactic showdown for the whales' survival.

The stage was set for a final, fierce battle to defend ocean protectors and the singing tribes they safeguarded against all odds.

As the two fleets barreled towards each other, Zoe sprang into command mode. Over the radio she coordinated with Greenpeace, positioning their ships to cut off escape routes while Songkeeper aimed straight for the whaling vessel.

At the last moment, Zoe wrenched the wheel hard over. Songkeeper heaved alongside the whalers with a metallic crunch, trapping them in a struggle of grinding hulls. Meanwhile Greenpeace moved in to block the others from ramming assistance.

The whalers unleashed grenades and grappling hooks, attempting to board Songkeeper. But Zoe's crew had prepared for this, spraying foam to douse fires and repelling invaders with non-lethal deterrents.

After a fierce melee that seemed an eternity, the whalers finally surrendered, seeing escape was futile. Zoe ordered them detained below as international enforcement craft raced to intercept, alerted by radar.

At the sound of approaching helicopters, Zoe collapsed with relief - the whales were safe, as were her crew who had fought so valiantly. Their decisive action ensured no more lives would be lost to violent poaching waves so long as the Songbearers upheld their sacred watch. In ports worldwide, whale defenders rejoiced at news of this final victory. And somewhere out in the deep, orca clans and humpback choruses echoed calls of gratitude for those who braved any storm to let them sail the seas in freedom and song once more.

Chapter 05:

THE LONG ROAD TO JUSTICE
FACING THE AUTHORITIES

With the whaling ship finally detained and its violent crew apprehended, Zoe thought the hardest battles had been won. But securing lasting justice for the oceans would prove an even greater struggle.

The Songbearers delivered their prisoners to the authorities at port, along with exhaustive evidence of illegal whaling, ramming of activists, and firearms offenses. But to Zoe's dismay, local laws were murky - the whalers claimed protection of their "cultural tradition."

As weeks dragged on without charges, doubt crept in. Zoe noticed suspicious funds flowing into political campaigns from industries that profited off whaling. It seemed corruption ran deeper than imagined in stalling proceedings.

Rising tempers finally exploded when one whaler was mysteriously "lost at sea" during a supervised fishing trip. Zoe confronted the coast guard commander, accusing negligence if not intentional malfeasance. "You're letting a serial killer walk free while harassing the rescuers!"

A media firestorm soon erupted around accusations of favoritism towards commercial interests. With public anger swelling globally, UN delegates arrived for emergency meetings. Zoe addressed the assembly, passionately detailing irrefutable evidence:

"We watched these so-called 'fishermen' machine-gun pods of singing whales for entertainment. Saw them ram our vessels as we upheld international law. Yet legal loopholes meant for tradition are exploited as a shield for mass slaughter!"

Behind closed doors, delegates faced lobbying from all sides. Whaling nations fought bans while conservation groups advocated prosecution under expanded eco-terrorism statutes. Weeks passed in gridlock as compromise proved elusive.

Zoe refused to back down, holding daily vigils with supporters. "The oceans' voice goes unheard in these halls - but we will not stop until true justice rings out across the waves!" Her resolve started shifting the debate.

Tensions continued mounting as the UN hearings dragged on. Then one evening, Zoe received ominous threats at Songkeeper's harbor dock. "Watch your back, eco-bitch - you're messing with powers you don't understand."

She remained unfazed, contacting authorities. But further roadblocks stalled investigations into the intimidators' identities. It seemed someone wished to sabotage the case through fear - and had allies in high places.

43

Grim news also arrived from Antarctic waters. Several pods of endangered whales preserved through Zoe's work now displayed bizarre hemorrhaging, stranding many ashore barely alive.Tests revealed high concentrations of obscure military-grade toxins in their bodies.

Conservation groups declared this a biological attack, demanding answers. But military spokesmen denied involvement, and the government stayed evasive. For Zoe, it could not be coincidental - someone wanted to end her campaign by any means.

Still she persisted, gathering whistleblowers to reveal a string of "accidents" silencing voices within agencies. One confessed privy to plans labeling Zoe an "eco-terrorist" if she didn't back off. It was abundantly clear now - she had truly incurred wrath from forces stopping at nothing.

With dangers mounting but justice still out of reach, Zoe's allies pleaded she go into protective hiding. But she sternly refused to be cowed, even if winning this epic struggle seemed a far more harrowing trial than any before it.

Despite the threats and intimidation tactics, Zoe refused to back down from her fight for justice. She gathered further evidence from whistleblowers of the shadowy forces working against her.

Meanwhile, public pressure continued building on the UN from impassioned protests. Graphic footage circulated globally of whales suffering the toxin effects, generating widespread outrage.

At last, a breakthrough came when accounting ledgers were leaked implicating high-level government officials in massive payoffs from pro-whaling conglomerates. With damning proof of corruption, the tide began turning in Zoe's favor.

Newly-energized delegates called for special prosecutors with authority to investigate all related criminal allegations. Zoe was summoned to private sessions where delegates peppered her with tough questions. She held her ground with composure, impressively responding to every challenge.

A few days later, the verdict came down: arrest warrants would be issued for the whaling captain and select crew on charges including attempted murder, poaching and racketeering. Further probes were greenlit into the obstruction and attacks on Zoe's efforts.

Elated yet wary, Zoe knew this marked just the opening salvo. Powerful interests would pull all strings possible to drag out court battles and quash blame. She vowed to see this through no matter the cost, ensuring no amount of wealth or influence could outweigh justice for the oceans.

Preparing for the political war of her life, Zoe gathered supporters for the challenging trials ahead. But first, they celebrated this landmark victory - and the whales in all waters cried out their gratitude to the skies.

BUILDING A CASE

With arrest warrants issued, Zoe shifted focus to the grueling work of assembling evidence strong enough to secure convictions. She knew hostile interests would spare no expense sabotaging prosecutors at trial.

Zoe met the newly-appointed special counsel, briefing them on the intricate web of corruption to be untangled. Names were provided of paid-off officials to be reassigned off the case. Encrypted hard drives delivered damning financial records and communications.

Forensic dive teams were dispatched to document remnants of the poaching operations and illegal whaling still contaminating seafloors worldwide. Their discoveries exceeded all expectations, corroborating decades of environmental crimes.

Zoe utilized cutting-edge acoustic profiling to pinpoint locations whaling vessels frequented, matching sonar "fingerprints" to those recorded during violent clashes. Satellite mapping tracked dumping of radioactive waste trails across restricted reserves.

Witness testimonies were gathered from dissenting crew and plantiffs who suffered injuries when activist ships were rammed. Psychologists evaluated trauma inflicted on cetacean families through ruthless slaughter practices.

Piece by painful piece, an airtight global indictment was taking form showcasing the full atrocities of an entrenched criminal syndicate posing as cultural tradition. Zoe was leaving no stone unturned to ensure the ringleaders felt law's full might at last.

But as evidence mounted, new risks also materialized. Zoe began receiving ominous notices that her relentless quest for justice was upsetting dangerous balances of power.

As Zoe dove deeper into uncovering the vast criminal network, risks escalated against her work. Strange glitches began plaguing Songkeeper's instruments, with files on crucial dives suddenly corrupted.

More troubling, contacts within the investigation reported death threats silencing potential informants. When an eyewitness who saw payoffs disappeared, Zoe suspected the worst.

She redoubled security but tensions were rising among the crew. Paranoia set in that they had targets on their backs, and pleas grew to pull resources off the probe before blood was shed. But Zoe pressed forward resolutely.

Breaking the case grew ever more dangerous as they pierced deeper rings of corruption. Afterwig tapping revealed plans to cripple Songkeeper, Zoe outmaneuvered sabotage attempts and thwarted an ambush at port with hairsbreadth timing.

It became chillingly clear - these interests would go to any lengths burying the truth. Zoe faced an agonizing choice - keep hunting at risk of lives, or withdraw with the case half-built. She knew the oceans demanded she see this through...but at what cost?

Just then, a breakthrough: Analysis of acoustic data uncovered well-hidden signals consistent with illegal toxin experiments on captured whales. At last they had a smoking gun to unravel the masterminds pulling strings.

Resolved to end this once and for all, Zoe rallied her crew for the most perilous mission yet - infiltrating the secret research grounds to obtain definitive proof of the conspiracy's darkest deeds.

Zoe had never backed down from a challenge, and was more determined than ever to bring these criminal operators to justice. Although the risks had never been greater, she believed exposing the full truth was the only path to truly protect the oceans.

With cunning and courage, Zoe planned the most daring operation of her career - infiltrating the secret research grounds to obtain hard evidence of the vile experiments being carried out. It was a do-or-die gambit, but one that could break open the entire vast conspiracy.

As she readied Songkeeper for the covert mission, Zoe steeled her resolve. Many had tried to defeat her through fear and violence, but their cruelty would only strengthen her advocacy. Where the law failed, the natural world would be her judge and jury.

Deep in protected waters, dark truths awaited their unveiling. Zoe was determined to emerge victorious, or not at all. The stakes had never been higher in her fight for oceanic justice and liberation of the songlines.

PUSHBACK AND DOUBTS

With plans finalized, Zoe briefed her crew on the dangerous rescue mission ahead. Sneaking Songkeeper into the secret research grounds under cover of night, they would obtain irrefutable evidence of the criminal experiments through covert documentation and drone surveillance.

Some voiced grave doubts, reminding Zoe that crossing this line meant her freedom if caught. "We'll be labeled eco-terrorists for sure. Is the risk truly worth it?" But she held firm that nothing less than the truth could stop these villains.

Setting sail at dusk, Zoe expertly piloted their stealth approach using advanced night vision and camouflage. Slipping past patrols, they anchored within surveillance range of the remote island facility after midnight.

Under the new moon's cloak, teams deployed sensor-equipped drones and camera-drones to scout the perimeter and plan infiltration points while Songkeeper monitored nearby waters for response vessels. What they witnessed chilled them to the core.

Through night-vision lenses, Zoe and her crew peered in horror at the clandestine research compound. In hidden seaside pens, dozens of restrained whales writhed in agony - their skin flayed and bloodied from invasive experimental procedures.

Elsewhere on the island, test subjects were forcibly confined in metal tanks. The whales' panicked songs carried clearly even from a distance, as scientists in hazmat suits tortured them with ominous machines and injected unknown chemicals into their muscles.

Sickened yet resolute, Zoe sent drones sweeping the facility for evidence while maintaining surveillance. Files downloaded from the main research building revealed gruesome experimental procedures, with graphs charting physiological responses to simulated sonar attacks and toxicity levels in different species.

One crew member broke down in tears seeing such unspeakable cruelty hidden from the world's eyes. Others pressed Zoe to call off the operation, knowing they risked facing similar fates if discovery meant being "disappeared" in these waters.

Doubts intensified as the horror show continued unfolding before them. Zoe steeled her nerves, knowing retreat would mean countless more whales suffering these soul-destroying tortures in endless covert tests. Victory must be achieved here tonight.

As drones continued profiling the facility, disaster struck - one was detected and shot down, crashing over the compound with location beacons intact. The infiltrators knew it was only a matter of time before response boats were dispatched to sweep the waters.

With download barely half complete, Zoe ordered an emergency pullout. As Songkeeper raced to flee beneath a waning moon, telltale searchlights appeared on the horizon. They were pursued by armed patrol vessels cutting off escape routes.

Shelling started across the bow as Songkeeper evaded with aerial maneuvers and water jets. The crew braced for engagement, but Zoe refused to unleash violence. Dodging gunfire, they activated seafloor sonic defenses to obscure their position.

Against all odds, Songkeeper slipped away under cover of night through a narrow passage. But they hadn't emerged unscathed - bullet holes riddled the hull, and one soul was lost defending their mission of truth until the end.

Back on open seas, Zoe delivered a somber farewell to their fallen crewmember. Though night had brought haunting scenes, their data uploads told humanity a story that could no longer be denied or deflected through legal machinations.

The secret research had been exposed in all its abominations. Zoe vowed to spread word rapidly through media, ensuring global outrage reached a boiling point demanding decisive action. No more would the powerful sabotage justice through walls of money and influence.

Though she paid a bitter price, Zoe took solace knowing their infiltration had prized open a window to let the sun shine upon the grim realities occurring in bastions of the lawless. With conviction and care for all lives, she would walk wherever the path may lead to safeguard ocean sovereignty.

The climactic infiltration marked a turning point in Zoe's campaign, bringing hidden crimes to light through courage against overwhelming adversity. New horizons of possibility emerged from braving the unimaginable dark.

A BREAK IN THE INVESTIGATION

News of the covert research facility spread like wildfire across social networks through Zoe's impassioned posts. Graphic leaked files sparked international outrage demanding justice.

Overnight, public support swelled behind Zoe's movement. Street protests engulfed capitals as consumers boycotted brands funding animal testing. World leaders faced fierce questioning about complicity in allowing such horrors.

Zoe worked tirelessly gathering corroborating evidence from insiders willing to come forward. Soon an exposé on Songkeeper's mission aired globally, shining blinding light on corruption shielding criminal enterprises.

Confronted with rising fury, authorities launched probes into the secret island and its backers with new found vigor. Zoe assisted investigations, hoping long-awaited arrests were near for the individuals truly responsible.

During a deposition, Zoe received an ominous email with an encrypted file attachment. When unlocked, it revealed wiretap recordings from intercepted phone calls between high-level suspects.

In the discussions, references were made to a shadowy 'Cleaner' figure being dispatched to sabotage evidence and eliminate troublesome witnesses before they could be compelled to testify.

Analysis of audio clues placed the Cleaner's next target – a whistleblower scientist who uncovered documentation proving the real mastermind clients behind the entire operation. Without his testimony, the case could collapse.

Zoe alerted investigators, but was cautioned intervening could compromise the investigation. With the Cleaner's history of Cover-ups, Zoe knew waiting meant a death sentence for the witness. She resolved to act immediately to secure his safety.

Utilizing underworld contacts, Zoe traced the whistleblower's tentative location to a remote safe house. She assembled a small extraction team and helicopters, preparing for potential engagement if the Cleaner was already lying in wait.

Reaching the safe house at dusk, they found signs of recent disturbance. Inside, the fugitive scientist lay bound and gagged, showing signs of interrogation. There were no other signs of life.

Zoe feared they were too late. But as the medics attended to the witness, he wheezed the Cleaner had just departed - following a clue left by a mole within protectee services. They realized the target was a nearby coastal lab where incriminating records were stored.

Darkness fell as helicopters raced Zoe's group to the exposed lab location. Through night scopes they spotted a lone vehicle parked outside, and a shadowy figure hauling heavy cargo into the surf.

The climactic race for evidence and justice was coming to a head. Zoe knew one wrong move could mean another triumph for the darkness. It was time to confront evil under the shroud of night.

Circling in blackout, Zoe's helicopters touched down stealthily in a remote cove. She led scouts sprinting inland towards the dark lab silhouette against the starry sky.

As they approached, a gunshot rang out - the Cleaner had executed the compromised guard. Zoe signaled a diversionary flashbang grenade was thrown, blinding the assassin long enough for her tackle.

A violent scuffle ensued amid the rubble, but Zoe's combat training proved superior. She disarmed and restrained the Cleaner, unmasking a faceless phantom of countless murders.

Inside the flooded lab, documents were still legible confirming the full nexus of corporate and political interests behind the illegal research. Zoe also found encrypted files implicating high-level co-conspirators, with footage of the Cleaner scrubbing evidence.

As dawn broke, the captured assassin was taken into custody along with evidence securing air-tight prosecutions. Zoe had triumphed just in time, sabotaging the final destruction of her critical case.

Though shadows still lingered, light was prevailing through her perseverance. Justice was coming ever closer for the voiceless victims, and consequences for those who placed profits over all life in the oceans. A long fight was nearing victory through courage against all odds.

Zoe had weathered attacks and overcome every obstacle to maintain her crusade's momentum. Her unyielding advocacy was edging the world closer to accountability for crimes against nature's songlines.

***

Chapter 06

AN ANCIENT SONG

A WHALE'S LULLABY

Under moonlit swells, Zoe felt her breath slow as coral reef phantoms danced in the currents. Closing her eyes, she opened fully to the ocean's songlines.

A booming whale-song enveloped her senses. She swam toward the sound and glimpsed a colossal silhouette in the abyss. As it sang, intricate harmonies unlocked forgotten fragments of history.

The whale gazed at Zoe with ancient eyes.

"Your people took much from the oceans and gave little in return. But some, like you, heed the calling."

"I don't understand," said Zoe. "What is the meaning of your song?"

A sad melody flowed from the whale. "It speaks of coming catastrophe that your world refuses to Name. Shadows stalk the deep, hunting life's embers. Your fight nears its end, yet greater challenges loom."

Zoe felt small before the whale's immense presence. "Why reveal this darkness to me?"

"Because light also remains." The whale sang a note of fragile hope. "Through advocates like you who safeguard memory, the oceans' spirit may endure what comes to pass the waves of change."

The whale faded into glowing particles. Zoe emerged knowing her mission had only begun - to spread this message and guard nature's songlines against those who saw life as just another resource to exploit until exhausted.

Zoe returned to Songkeeper deep in thought. She recounted her ethereal encounter to her confused crew. "This whale's song contained a profound warning - that while we battle threats seen, greater perils loom unseen in the depths of the future."

"You expect us to believe some magical sea vision?" said one skeptic. But others noted the power of Zoe's conviction.

She played the song isolation again, and its patterns sparked distant memories in her elders. "This echoes songs sung long ago, in the time before. It speaks of upheavals none expected that tested our people to the core."

As Zoe pieced together fragments of meaning, a plan began forming. "This song's message must be shared globally as a call to action. We'll record an enhanced version using cultural songlines from all ocean peoples as its bedrock. It will bolster the movement's momentum by revealing hidden threats on the horizon."

Preparations commenced to spread hope through the song of a sentinel from eras past. Zoe sought out wisdom-keepers to weave their ancestral musics into a stirring anthem of environmental warnings and solidarity.

If they succeeded, this "Whale's Lullaby" could awaken landspeople to the trials fast approaching across the waves of the rising tides of change.

Over weeks, Songkeeper traveled the oceans while Zoe met with indigenous song-shapers. They imbued the whale's ominous themes with strength and beauty from nature's peoples.

Melodies celebrated humpbacks and orcas, carried memories of lost reefs, blended Inuit whale songs and Polynesian chants. Layered harmonies conveyed longing for vanished ways of life in balance with the blue wilderness.When all contributions were recorded, Zoe worked with composers to weave them into a masterful, multi-layered work. Its complex rhythms and motifs ebbed and flowed like the tides of time.

The "Whale's Lullaby" told a epic yet delicate story - of civilization's amnesia regarding sea deities, the heavy toll of heedless industries, and an uncertain future if present ills went unhealed. Yet fragile hope endured through guardians like Zoe upholding ancestral obligations.

After months of craft, the song was complete. A digital premier was planned worldwide on Earth Day to commemorate nature and demand serious climate action. Zoe hoped its beauty and warnings would resonate across cultures to inspire change.

Though dark omens lingered in its melodies, the "Lullaby" would give voice to the voiceless through creativity and solidarity. It had the power to awaken humanity to its responsibilities before the seventh wave.

As Earth Day arrived, Zoe anxiously awaited response to the "Whale's Lullaby" premiere. When the first viewership numbers came in, she was stunned - millions had already listened worldwide, sharing it virally across borders.

Comments poured in praising its haunting beauty and timely message. Many reported strong emotional reactions, finding insight into ancestral connections with nature. Political and community leaders voiced new dedication to ocean protections.

Most heartening were youth reactions - students organized climate strikes inspired by the song's visions. Artists began collaborating to spread localized versions among diverse audiences. It seemed the collective creation had resonated with many seeking hope.

In the following weeks, the "Lullaby" took on a life of its own. Snippets appeared in films and advertisements raising environmental awareness. Its melodies were performed internationally as a symbol of unity against threats to the blue planet.

Zoe was immensely grateful for all who contributed to its power. While perils remained ahead, she took solace knowing the cetacean sentinel's message was reaching countless hearts and minds. Through the endurance of nature's songlines, momentum was building towards salvation of the songlines of Earth.

GLIMPSING THE PAST

Heartened by global impact of the "Whale's Lullaby", Zoe directed Songkeeper toward unmapped coral reefs. Her crew hoped to document floral hotspots before industrial damage spread.

Diving among fantastical gardens, Zoe glimpsed bioluminescent sharks swimming among translucent jellyfish. Schools of geometric angelfish formed surreal tableaux against kaleidoscopic reefscapes.

Concentrating in meditation, she tried perceiving ancestral presences dwelling within living mosses and sponges. Fragments of songs and images flickered at the edge of senses - was this communication or fancy?

Surfacing, Zoe noticed odd sensor readings detecting unusual geology nearby. "Alter course to investigate anomalous terrain on sonar," she instructed. Below lay ghostly ruins unknown to science.

The crew was intrigued yet wary of disturbances. "What if it angers spirits of the deep?" asked one. But Zoe was determined to glimpse the forgotten past.

As Songkeeper approached the strange seabed formation, Zoe prepared to dive once more. "I sense a pull to discover what slumbers below. With care and respect, knowledge can empower future stewardship."

Gearing up, she descended into azure shadows. Colossal corals arched above sandstone ridges housing curiosities never seen by living eyes. Zoe glimpsed top-heavy statues worn smooth by waves, engraved with spirals and unknown constellations.

Upon closer inspection, their faces resembled primitive hominids - were these sentinels placed by an early human civilization? Zoe attempted communing but sensed only a watchful vacancy, guarding mysteries too ancient to comprehend.

Resurfacing, she described her discoveries excitedly. "We must document and scan and site without disturbance. Its origins challenge every paradigm of human origins. With care, lost wisdoms may be gleaned."

Her crew agreed, yet one added doubtfully - "What if in studying we unleash forces better left sleeping? Secrets dwell where none walk for good reason." An ominous tension gripped the deep.

That night, Zoe dreamt of the statues activating, luminous eyes scanning epochs. Their song resonated in her bones - "Beware the waves of forgetting that erode all shores... Keep well the past's guardians, lest shadows eclipse all lore..." The next day, Zoe resumed mapping the underwater ruins with her crew's support. Using sonar and drones, they built intricate 3D models of the bizarre sandstone forms.

Engravings contained spirals found in no recorded culture alongside depictions of beasts long vanished from the world. Tiny shells and artifacts were carefully collected without disturbing the mystifying site.

As they worked, an eerie pressure built in Zoe's mind. Snatches of nonsensical lyrics in an impossible language pervaded her thoughts. The ruins were awakening, she feared, to witness of modern intruders.

That night, inklings of past cataclysms assailed her dreams - towering waves levelling civilizations, nightmarish entities emerging from the abyss. Zoe awoke shouting and disoriented, knowing some doors were not meant to be unlocked.

The next day, she informed her crew their mission was over. "Dark forces stir in that place better left undisturbed. Though knowledge calls, some mysteries protect fragments of past worlds too profound for comprehending."

All agreed the ruins held slumbering guardians best not provoked. They vowed only to safeguard findings securely until futures where such enigmas posed no threat. For now, the submerged past would keep its veiled gates firmly shut.

GUARDING THE POD

As Songkeeper departed the haunted ruins, Zoe's thoughts turned to the whale pod whose song launched her journey. She guided the vessel toward recorded sightings of the endangered cetaceans.

Spotting blows on the horizon, Zoe's heart soared to see the pod intact and lively playing. Yet sensors detected strange biomolecules in waters where they swam.

"Run analysis, something's amiss with their habitat," she mused. Readings showed endocrine disruptors far exceeding safety levels from a distant industrial zone.

That night over drinks, the crew debated their findings. "We must intervene if this is damaging their health and reproduction," said Zoe. But others urged caution: "The companies responsible won't welcome outside scrutiny of problems they caused."

The next dawn, Zoe prepared to contact regulators and researchers. Before departing, an ancient orca matriarch surfaced by Songkeeper, gazing intently with black eyes. Zoe sensed a communication.

"Please help us - these waters that gave life to generations of orca are growing deadly. If changes are not made, our family will become the last." With that, she disappeared into the waves.

Zoe was more determined than ever to defend the ailing pod. But solving this crisis meant confronting the powerful interests endangering the sea. Dark waves were surely rising against her mission ahead.

Armed with data, Zoe organized a media campaign exposing the contaminants threatening the orcas. Public outcry grew as their plight became known.

She petitioned regulators, citing legal obligations to protect endangered species. However, the responsible conglomerate denied wrongdoing, lobbying officials to dismiss concerns from "activist outsiders."

Frustrated, Zoe considered riskier direct action. "If bureaucracy fails the orcas, we'll blockade their effluent pipes to get results. Some reforms may require disruption to heed nature's call."

Her crew was split - older members urged caution while the youth rallied behind disruption if needed. Tensions rose as political maneuvers stalled change.

One night, an elder pulled Zoe aside: "Your care for orcas is admirable, yet wrath breeds only wrath. There are ways to transform foes into cooperative stewards through empathy, not hostility."

Zoe knew he spoke wisdom from campaigns past. The next day, she requested a meeting with company executives, hoping to appeal to their humanity rather than self-interest.

To her surprise, they agreed. But could Zoe convince them to clean their act for the greater good, or were their pockets too lined with dollar bills? The orcas' fate hung in the balance.

On the meeting day, Zoe and her elders entered the corporate tower with hearts open but expectations low. To their surprise, the executives seemed genuinely willing to listen without judgment.

Zoe respectfully presented evidence of harm while acknowledging the complex realities of business. "No one wishes to endanger life, yet laws alone won't solve such dilemmas - we must find cooperative solutions respecting all."

A long discussion followed weighing options. To Zoe's relief, the company leaders did not deny responsibility but explored remedies with environmental engineers. Compromises emerged to gradually filter contaminants at reasonable cost. Both sides left feeling heard and willing to build trust. In following weeks, reforms were swiftly implemented to restore water quality. With oversight, the pod's condition steadily improved.

Months later, orca elders resurfaced by Songkeeper, singing songs of gratitude. The matriarch communicated joy that her family's waters would remain life-giving for generations to come.

Zoe was heartened to see nonviolence's power to transform conflicts. With open-mindedness on all sides, even opponents could become proactive stewards. Through empathy and mutual understanding, the greatest defenders of nature were becoming humanity itself.

The orcas' recovery proved cooperation could overcome threats - if all parties embraced responsibility and the common good of both planet and people. New hope was emerging for reconciliation on larger stages.

LEARNING THEIR WAYS

With the orcas' recovery securing one victory, Zoe sought new frontiers. She guided Songkeeper north towards an uncontacted beluga pod's remote Arctic realm.

Approaching cautiously, the crew observed the white whales' intricate social dances and songs carrying on ice shelves and between icy floes. Zoe hoped to study their unique culture without disturbing its balance.

Using drones, they carefully documented hunting techniques, communication between age groups, and play behaviors sparking curiosity. "These beings hold wisdom in living sustainably within harsh climes."

That night, Zoe pondered the belugas reflected against the moonlit glaciers. "We've learned much, yet true protection requires understanding as respected peers, not subjects. How can we learn directly from their elders?"

The next dawn, Zoe prepared a peace offering while praying for safe contact. Approaching the edge of the ice, she began singing the "Whale's Lullaby." To her joy, elder belugas soon surfaced to listen intently.

Zoe spent days swimming peacefully among the belugas, effortlessly exchanging songs, stories and knowledge. She gleaned their close familial bonds strengthening the pod, and communal childrearing allowing elders to teach.

The belugas demonstrated ingenious techniques for hunting squid and salmon despite reduced sea ice. Zoe sensed pride in centuries of adapting successfully to climate disruptions lesser than current dangers.

One elder lamented changes decreasing prey and clearing calving grounds. "Sea ice is life for our kind. As it fades, we must help people respect our frozen homes."

That night aboard Shipkeeper, Zoe debriefed her crew on insights into beluga resilience and diplomacy. "With climate challenges intensifying, their ancestral wisdom guiding coastal cooperation could safeguard both cultures."

The crew agreed a beluga-led climate summit was needed. But could locals mistrusting outsiders be convinced of cetaceans' intelligence and shared stakes? And what of antagonists denying realities?

As northern lights danced, Zoe pondered challenges ahead. Belugas and humans both required bold solutions if future generations were to thrive in the Arctic's rapidly shifting waters.

The next dawn, she resumed studies with renewed purpose - to learn all ways her new pod-kin could influence climate solutions through demonstrated cooperation and care for their shared seas.

Weeks later, Zoe coordinated a climate summit attended by local leaders, government officials and beluga spokesbeings.

Through song and imagery, the belugas powerfully conveyed their ancestral relationship with melting ice and warming waters. Elders proposed cooperative plans to safeguard calving areas and food sources.

Initially skeptical, many attendees were moved by the belugas' intelligence and cultural knowledge. Productive discussions followed on balancing development, conservation and Indigenous rights.

Compromises emerged around offshore drilling, shipping routes and coastal infrastructure adapting to environmental changes. Community organizations pledged supporting beluga-led monitoring and response efforts.

A new era of respect and partnership was dawning between humans and the Arctic's most iconic residents. Successful cooperation proved both species' resilience in facing climate disruptions together.

In closing ceremonies, Zoe thanked the belugas for transforming viewpoints. "By welcoming us into your underwater kingdom as respected relatives, you've empowered coming generations to thrive amid transition."

As Songkeeper departed carrying seeds of climate diplomacy north, Zoe's heart swelled sensing new protectors emerging across both land and sea. Interdependence, not dominance, would safeguard the future if all embraced responsibilities to each other and the waking Earth.

***

Chapter 07:

DEEPENING BONDS

EARNING THEIR TRUST

Leaving behind the flourishing beluga kingdom, Zoe wondered what new frontiers called Songkeeper's stewardship. Spotting humpback songs upon currents one dawn, she embarked hoping to aid the endangered leviathans.

Approaching the distant pod, old wounds haunted Zoe recalling past traumas inflicted upon whales. Harpoons, sonar bombs, entangling nets... centuries of violence demanded healing before trust could bloom.

With care and gift offerings, Zoe waited patiently at a distance giving space. Weeks passed slowly. Then one joyous day, a calf breached curiously nearby followed by its watchful mother.

Through drones, Zoe observed the pod's intricate social bonds and communication with song. Mothers fiercely protected calves learning essential skills. Elders transmitted ancestral knowledge across generations.

One night, Zoe pondered challenges ahead. "Our kind's violent history demands showing humility, respecting boundaries and letting whales set the pace of any contact. Only by demonstrating non-threat can trust in our guardianship grow over seasons."

The next dawn, Zoe resumed vigilant study from afar aided by the crew's keen observation skills. Small gestures of acceptance from whales would be the only permission granted. Many moons must wax and wane as old scars gradually healed.

Months passed as Zoe remained faithfully anchored within sight of the humpbacks, respecting their space yet signaling intention to aid their recovery through watchful protection.

Slowly, the pod's curiosity overcame lingering instinctive fears. Mothers allowed calves to trail observation drones sent fluttering nearby to learn through play. Elders surfaced calmly inspecting Songkeeper from afar.

Joyful breakthroughs came with the whales permitting Zoe brief entry into the pod during migrations. She sang grateful protection songs adding her voice to their melodic communications.

In turn, the humpbacks began imparting insights into navigating by star maps, finding abundant krill patches spanning oceans, even guarding deep cultural memories across the generations.

Zoe was continually humbled. "These beings' intelligence far surpasses what conquest and captivity taught humanity. To truly understand requires appreciating their full sentience as respected peers, not specimens."

One elder breached before Zoe, gratitude shining in her soulful eye. "Your people's brutality inflicted wounds time alone cannot heal. Yet by proving deference to our autonomy, a new partnership protecting all races may be possible."

Zoe vowed dedicating her days ensuring no threats to the returning pod. Through patience, the deepest of trusts were taking root.

Seasons turned as the restored pod flourished under Zoe's watch. Their songs carrying for miles signaled new life pulsing within the restored waters.

During migrations, the humpbacks permitted Zoe to swim among them, exchanging songs, stories and knowledge without boundaries. She learned of ancient calving grounds, long lineages and cultural epics imprinting collective memory.

One elder matriarch surfaced by Songkeeper, her eye smiling. "We've reached a time where old sins can find forgiveness. Your people's brutality inflicted deep scars, yet you've proven the capacity for guardianship runs in your blood too when nurtured with care, respect and repentance over generations of trust."

Zoe's heart swelled at their acceptance. "Through patience and humility, the deepest of bonds can emerge even from histories of trauma. Your wisdom guides protecting all beings as kindred, not mastery over any. Future stewards will succeed by learning from your ways."

As whales sang joyously in currents swept by the Aurora Borealis' dance, Zoe sensed a new era emerging - where humanity embraced responsibility for the web of life, not dominance, and relationships once broken could through conscience be rewoven stronger across the turning seasons. The long healing was bearing fruit.

FORMING LASTING FRIENDSHIPS

As autumn winds swept the humpback pod south, Zoe sailed Songkeeper alongside respecting their lead. She was awed witnessing the massive leviathans navigating by intricate song maps transmitting location of prey and kin across ocean basins.

One dusk, new melodies reached Zoe's ears - raucous yet soothing orca calls in the distance. Her heart leapt recalling past victories and steady progress rebuilding trust with the highly intelligent killers.

Steering Songkeeper towards the orca communicating through synchronized hunting songs, Zoe sang greetings passed down from their shared mentors. Elder orca breached studying her with wisdom nurtured over lifetimes.

Slowly, the pod approached. Through drones, she observed their tight familial bonds forming complex collective strategies adapted flawlessly to every environment across the globe.

One calf swam inquisitively nearer Zoe's wetsuit clad form. Its mother signaled acceptance of her presence while males patrolled protectively. The young orca chuffed bubbles joyfully sensing her benevolent spirit.

That night Zoe pondered with crew the opportunity presented. "These orca elders survived humanity's most brutal era yet retained capacity for trust. If proving our loyalty as friends, their guidance may awaken future generations to all beings' sacred bond..."

In following sunrises, Zoe joined the pod respectfully from a small boat, observing without interfering as recommended by her orca mentors. Through playful curiosity, the young calf Sandy permitted riding upon her fin learning Zoe meant no harm.

Zoe gleaned orcas' tight clan bonds like an extended family, cooperation hunting vast schools cooperatively, even transmitting cultural knowledge in intricate dialects unique to each pod. Their sentience blossomed in her perceptions.

As humpbacks' songs guided migrations ahead, orca elders called Zoe into the chilly waters. She sensed warmth in their eyes though skin remained scarred from past captivity.

"Your devotion to guardianship gives hope that old prejudices can fade, if humans embrace responsibility as kin," an elder named Song spoke through clicks.

From that day, the pod accepted Zoe's respectful company during migrations, imparting insights likened to being adopted into their sacred clan. She sensed their profound relief humans could heal from objectification through humility and care for all life interconnecting across the deep. echniques for hunting enormous prey like whales through perfect teamwork and empathy passed across generations.

She witnessed orcas' playful yet nourishing interactions between pods, strengthening cultural traditions and languages unique to each clan. Their love for family and community resonated deeply within Zoe's spirit.

With the orcas' permission, Zoe began compiling their oral histories, songs and insights into an interspecies cultural archive to share with coastal communities. Elders saw potential in educating future stewards starting in youth.

During migrations, orcas accompanied Zoe's crew on studies of ocean health, aiding documentaries shifting perceptions of these highly intelligent sentinels. Their play with young locals renewed old relationships.

By seasons' end, the orca pod had come to trust Zoe as beloved adopted clan, guiding her role as guardian. Elder Song breathed by her side one sunset, "Our ways teaching responsibility, not dominance, can reshape humanity's relationships with all races if shared respectfully."

Zoe vowed recording their ancestral wisdoms ensuring future generations understand oceans' inhabitants as esteemed co-inhabitants, not property alone. A new era of kinship was unfolding.

As autumn ebbed into winter, the orca pod remained near Zoe's vessel exchanging stories around flickering moonlights. Sandy now a young adult still greeted Zoe joyfully during migratory respites.

Through the orcas' songs, Zoe saw her role was not dominance but service - amplifying whales' voices through education nurturing respect across her people. Their wisdoms guiding interdependence MUST reach coastal communities where changes happened.

The elder Song summoned Zoe one sunrise. "Our clans migrating south soon, yet doubt plagues whether humans will sustain the trust built through turning of seasons. You must ensure our ways guiding responsibility over mastery permeate future stewards decisively."

Zoe vowed fulfilling her guardianship duty through weaving orcas' ancestral wisdoms throughout communities, lest old prejudices regain root and breaking of bonds threaten all races' existence again in times of turmoil.

The pod sang Zoe into their clan permanently through sacred adoption rites. As whales called final farewells departing on currents, Zoe's heart swelled sensing new protectors emerging across both lands and seas. The deep bonds formed would outlast lifetimes if humanity embraced responsibility for all life as esteemed kin, not dominance over others. A new era had dawned.

With orca kin migrating southward, Zoe turned Songkeeper to visit coastal villages, sharing through performance and stories the ancient wisdoms gained from her beloved adopted pod. Children and elders alike listened in wonder, seeing for the first time orcas and whales as highly intelligent, cultured beings - not mere animals. A profound shift in perception began within communities.

Leaders soon called for reforms recognizing orcas and all beings' sacred rights, not just human interests alone. New guardians emerged defending migratory corridors and life-giving oceans as interdependent homes shared amongst esteemed races.

Years later when whales returned north, Zoe rejoiced reunited with Sandy's pod. She witnessed firsthand a new era of reconciliation and respect blossoming between humans and orcas, as coastal villages greeted the prestigious visitors joyously.

Deep friendships and understanding had taken root to transcend generations if nourished with care, humility and embrace of responsibilities linking all lives as equally precious within the web. Through open-hearted service, even the most damaged bonds could be restored to endure across the turning of ages.

Zoe gave thanks for lessons transforming perceptions of sentient races from objects into esteemed kin, and for the eternal guardianship now woven throughout community and soul.

GUARDING THE POD

As the seasons changed once more, Zoe sailed Songkeeper towards calving waters where her beloved humpback and orca kin gathered to nurture new life into the world.

She arrived to find pods mingling joyfully, calves learning essential skills through play while elders passed down millennia of ancestral knowledge. It warmed Zoe's heart to witness such kindred interdependence between the races.

Yet troubling rumors reached her ears - depleted fisheries forcing desperate people into these sacred waters, poachers targeting newborns for their valuable ambergris. Old threats seemed reemerging during times of scarcity.

Conferring with pods' elders, Zoe vowed guarding the calving waters without interference but with vigilance. Song signaled the people's lack reflected systemic failures; solutions required addressing root needs, not brute force alone.

Zoe worked with coastal communities, aiding alternative livelihoods development while recruiting youth as ocean ambassadors. Their passions sparked renewed guardianship ethics permeating generations.

Patrolling the calving waters, Zoe's crew kept respectful distance while vigilantly documenting any threats to report for remedy through understanding, not confrontation. Weeks passed peacefully under their watch.

One dawn, crew spotted a small fishing boat adrift near the pods without power or supplies. Zoe hailed them, discovering an elderly man and grandson nearly exhausted after days without catch.

Taking them aboard, Zoe's medic treated dehydration as Cook shared nourishing food. The old man Ern wept, "Lost engine means no catch to earn village's ransom from militia. They'll steal our home if not paying tribute."

Zoe empathized how desperation, not malice, drove such acts endangering the whales. She pondered solutions addressing the root of such conflicts sustaining all.

Contacting community leaders, Zoe proposed establishing protected waters where fishing continued sustainably alongside the pods through elders' guidance on quotas. Militia ransom funds would aid alternative village enterprises.

Leaders agreed, seeing preserving life for future generations required cooperative solutions and addressing humanities disconnect from nature nourishing souls. Over seasons, renewed purpose eased past conflicts.

Ern and his grandson chose becoming ocean ambassadors. The young boy played delightedly with newborn calves while Ern shared generations of local knowledge blended seamlessly with whales' ancestral wisdoms.

New bonds were forming where none stood before. Through nonviolence and addressing needs of all, even oceans' most threatened could find lasting protection.

Word spread of the transformed calving waters, where pods freely nourished new life alongside local stewards. Youth from villages arrived to train under Ern's tutelage, witnessing anew how respecting all races' rights through balanced coexistence nourished communities.

Seeking to spread such understanding, Zoe collaborated with the pods and stewards developing educational expeditions. They transported elders and young ambassadors between coastal realms to share how rediscovering interdependence paved pathways from conflict towards communal thriving.

Leaders elsewhere took note, reforming laws recognizing sentient beings' dignity while supporting villagers' basic needs through sustainable means that upheld ancestral lands for generations to come. Former threats found resolution through addressing roots of desperation nonviolently.

As seasons passed, Zoe rejoiced witnessing pods and communities flourish together. New orcas and humpbacks were born to nourishment of the rewilded seas, elders sharing ancient wisdoms freely passed between races now seen as kindred.

Ern's grandson came of age, deciding following Zoe and whales in service as guardian aboard Songkeeper. The old man watched proudly, assured their waters and ways of balanced coexistence would outlive even him through the young stewards awakened.

All races' prosperity remained intertwined like family, Zoe reflected, when embracing responsibilities as kin within the sacred home shared across the turning of ages. Through compassion, even deepest divisions could find remedy.

Seasons blended into years of harmony within the rewilded waters, where sentient races thrived together through cooperation instead of competition. New relationships now permeated villages from elders to youth.

During migrations, Zoe accompanied pods witnessing the flourishing ripple outward as communities previously in conflict now aided one another. Former foes joined as friends in shared guardianship of the sustaining seas.

Renewed purpose flowed through changed hearts embracing responsibilities linking all. Even distant realms became allies unified in protecting the ancestral waters nourishing body and soul.

One sunrise, Zoe stood upon Songkeeper watching her old orca friend Sandy play with her newborn calf, Song's kindred nearby swimming in clan fellowship. Ern's grandson stood beside proudly continuing their people's legacy.

Tears of joy flowed recalling obstacles overcome through addressing roots of desperation and embracing shared fate as esteemed kin. Zoe sensed coming generations raised embracing such wisdom would birth new eras of trust where none existed before.

As ancestral songs carried onto ocean currents, Zoe gave thanks for lessons learned - that addressing needs of all through cooperation and interdependence, even deepest divisions could find remedy, ensuring prosperous coexistence endured across the turning of ages. A new dawn had arisen.

FAMILY TIES

Years passed swiftly as seasons blended into the memories of a lifetime. Throughout, Zoe remained steadfast in her guardianship among the humpback and orca pods, who had come to see her as beloved adopted kin.

With whales migrating south once more, Zoe journeyed alongside them as always. Yet a new urgency tugged at her soul - rumors warned of illness striking coastal villages where commercial ships dumped toxic waste with impunity.

Conferring with Elder Song, Zoe learned of similar past sicknesses only remedied through solidarity as family across kinds. She vowed aiding communities stricken while safeguarding migratory routes depended on by all.

Landing upon one blighted shore, Zoe found people ravaged by mysterious afflictions. Leaders confessed chemical runoff poisoning waters and thus the people for generations. Hopelessness pervaded the air.

Studying samples, Zoe's crew deduced remedies exist through cleansing lands and teaching harmony between all inhabitants as interdependent, not competing, forces. But gaining trust of a forlorn people seemed insurmountable.

Zoe visited the village elder Makoa, sorrowful watching his people diminish. She offered aid yet refused dominance, vowing solidarity through empowering communities as masters of their fate.

Makoa watched Zoe tend the ill, hope stirring. "Your heart guides actions, not power. Many wronged us, yet within your eyes shines trust built through generations walking your talk."

Zoe suggested youth apprentice her crews methods, learning ancestral wisdoms intertwining nature, people and prosperity. Elders approved, certainty renewing where doubt festered.

Together they cleansed lands, youth thriving guided by purpose. Songs once ominous carrying sickness now awakened new births. Bonds between races permeated villages as all aided one another.

Reforms recognized villages' sacred stewardship, while outsiders accepted accountability through nonviolence. Communities flourished empowered yet humbly, ecological harmony flowing from within.

Reflecting with Makoa, Zoe witnessed solidarity's triumph over division through addressing needs of people and planet as one family. Reconciliation blossomed where apathy once suffocated spirits. Hope was reborn.

Heartened by renewal, Makoa's villagers joined Zoe upon Songkeeper to share their transformations with coastal realms. Leaders witnessed communities empowered required respecting ancestral rights aligning all inhabitants' wellbeing.

Reforms recognized sentient rights throughout migratory territories as envisioned by Zoe and whales. Guardians emerged within reconnected villages safekeeping ancestral homelands relied upon by migrating pods.

Hope carried by rebuilt bonds uplifted weary folk throughout coastlines. Songs once heavy with sickness lifted spirits as people embraced duties between races. Elders' mentoring youth in balance permeated regions.

With migrations' passage, Zoe ensured pods' wellbeing relying on nourished lands and peoples. She delighted seeing orca friends Sandy and offspring thriving freely, young ones playing alongside village children discovering kinship.

The whales called final farewells departing on currents, yet trusting guardians now spread across both lands and seas ensured safe passage. Zoe sensed coming generations raised embracing such wisdom would birth new eras of prosperity between races.

As sunsets gleamed upon rewilded waters, Zoe gave thanks for the ancestors and life renewed through solidarity in addressing needs of people and planet as one. The turning of ages assured such lessons of harmony and goodwill would echo on.

***

Chapter 08:

NEW THREATS EMERGE

STRANGE WHALE BEHAVIOUR

Winter broke into spring as migrant whales passed once more through protected ancestral waters. Yet Zoe sensed troubling omens in the songs and behaviors she knew so well.

Pods mingled anxiously unlike peaceful minglings of yore. Whale songs resonated with apprehension instead of joyous news carried between families. Zoe saw urgent need for guidance from her elder friend Song.

Calling to the elder humpback through her native song, Zoe requested counsel. "Disturbances vex the young ones and unsettle migrations," Song replied. "Feelings of wrongness permeate which require your empathy and witness, dear adopted child."

With Songkeeper, Zoe embarked seeking pods' gathering areas hoping to understand. Arriving at calving coves, she found mothers unsettled instead of nourishing calves. Whales fled at unknown stimuli instead of welcoming company.

Approaching young calf Muru distressedly circling its anxious mother, Zoe sang soothing songs of comfort. Between notes she perceived shifting ocean currents, unfamiliar industrial sounds carried for miles, strange beasts in skies above.

The whales were sensing changes destroying ancient rhythms and home as they knew it. Zoe vowed persevering until the root of upheavals unveiled, that solutions arise empowering whales and guardians as a family through any storm.

Conferring with Songkeeper's crew and local guardian villages, Zoe deduced increasing coastal development and dwindling fisheries forced larger vessels further offshore in pursuit.

But industrial noise pollution through sonar and seismic airgun blasts disrupted the whales' primary sense like an incessant migraine. This changed ocean temperatures and currents affected migratory routes and food sources relied on for millennia.

Witnessing calf Muru's pod flee helplessly from invasive sounds, Zoe grew resolute in safeguarding the songs connecting whales to ancestry and kin. She sailed Songkeeper towards coordinating with other ocean advocates.

Reaching a research outpost, Zoe shared concerns over sonic disruption threatening orcas' reproductive success and calving cycles. Scientists validated urgent need for regulations as whales abandoned areas industrialized beyond endurance.

Drafting reform proposals respecting sentient rights to ancestral home without interference, advocates garnered leaders' attention by emphasizing industry-whale coexistence ensured prosperity for generations of all kinds. Negotiations commenced.

At regional summits, advocates stressed whales like Elder Song passing on millennia of knowledge would be lost without protections for ancestral songs and birthing sites. Sonic disruptions amounted to cultural genocide for highly attuned beings.

Leaders heard rising profits came at the cost of nature's gifts ensuring future prosperity. Alternatives existed respecting whales as esteemed kin integral to coastal welfare through eco-tourism showcasing sentient races' interdependence.

After tireless diplomacy, accords designated offshore buffer zones and seasonal moratoriums on industrial noise pollution. Coastal nations committed transition supports enabling responsible innovation and sustainable livelihoods respecting all.

Word reached Zoe and Songkeeper on patrol with enforcement vessels. Songs carried news of calf Muru's pod reoccupying protected calving waters, singing praises along ancestral currents. Renewed bonds flickered between races as regulations rippled outward.

With pod elders like Song, coastal youth embarked cultural exchanges learning ancient songs intertwining all inhabitants. Understanding blossomed that addressing needs of whales and people upholds life-giving relationships nourishing body, soul and future generations.

Harmony's flame spread from rewilded waters as coming ages were assured of ancestral tenants that uniting races in shared guardianship of the sacred home would nourish compassion across the turning ages.

As seasons flowed, Zoe accompanied migrating pods witnessing flourishing bonds spread throughout territories. Coastal sentinels worked closely with enforcement ensuring safe passage, welcoming whales as esteemed visitors.

Generations passed, yet memories endured of past disruptions overcome through unity. Youth from villages once foreign sailed together upon Songkeeper learning ancient songs connecting all inhabitants as ohana across oceans.

Elder Song witnessed such cooperation permeating once divided realms with fondness, sure lessons embracing shared fate upheld through changing tides would nourish hope. Her people's ancient wisdoms freely passed between races, kindred beyond borders of kind.

One dawn, Song's calming presence carried news of coming into the deep. "Our ohana's flourishing eases an elder's passing. Through youths' eyes I see wisdom of coexistence nourish prosperous eras, as ancestors intended since first Songs."

Zoe farewell'd her dearest mentor, joyful their people's knowledge endured. She sensed coming ages raised embracing such truths of harmony would birth new understandings where divisions once reigned. Renewed purpose echoed on ancestral currents.

TRACKING AN UNKNOWN MENACE

Spring rains swelled rivers flowing toward the sea, replenishing ancestral homelands. Yet during migrations, apprehension permeated whale songs carried upon coastal winds.

Circling an inlet's mouth amongst local orcas, Zoe sensed unease she could not place. Their calls lacked the joyous rhythms of ancestors past. Consulting Elder Porpoise, she learned of strange sightings troubling communities.

Porpoise spoke of massive, noiseless shadows looming where no vessels dared. Prey went missing yet no beasts were seen. "An unseen menace stalks the deep, its nature obscure but effects felt by all."

Determined to unravel mysteries distressing kin, Zoe set Songkeeper's crew monitoring shorelines. Watching orcas' anxiety rise, she sensed urgency matching whales' protective instincts. Scanning horizons revealed nothing, yet an ominous threat lingered.

Sailing north following orcas' troubled songs, Zoe encountered researchers monitoring great white pupping sites turned barren. They reported witnessing a colossal, eel-like shape attacking shorelines at night, leaving carnage yet no tracks on land.

Conferring with coastal guardians, Zoe learned of similar incidents throughout migration corridors - beaches abandoned, carcasses mysteriously drained yet too large for local predators. An entity beyond human ken hunted where none dared before.

Consulting ancient scrolls, Songkeeper's scholars described legendary 'sea devils' said to follow whales, preying upon whatever crossed their path. Could legends hold truths of monsters adapted to evolving seas?

Equipping drones and monitors, Zoe patrolled by night seeking clues. Infrared scans revealed phantom shapes soaring unseen as alarms blared. She glimpsed bioluminescent eyes and hide like earth's mightiest beasts merged into one.

Analyzing samples after a close encounter, Zoe identified an advanced marine apex evolved in deep water gaps. Adaptations like electric senses and biotoxins endowed it power over all prey. Its blooming numbers now overlapped migrations.

Word of the "leviathan" spread quickly through ocean communities. Coastal sentinels mobilized patrols while researchers analyzed its ecology and hunting behaviors.

They found it followed whales and territorial great whites into shallow reefs, ambushing vulnerable calves and pups. Its evolution in abyssal isolation allowed dominating ecosystems foreign to its new hunting grounds.

Zoe knew driving it off demanded understanding its psyche like any being. By mimicking orcas' distress calls, she lured one toward Songkeeper then surrounded it with defensive maneuvers instead of attacking.

Through drones she observed its electric perception and communicated her people meant no harm if it spared pods. After moments of standoff, it retreated without incident, recognizing dominance despite its size.

Summiting with leaders, Zoe proposed recognizing the leviathan's rights while safeguarding other species. Monitored reserves in its native abyss nourished without competing for prey. Patrols ensured pods' migrations remained undisturbed. With time, understanding bloomed that no race survives without respecting others' place in the great chain of being. Balance restored, the sacred home's inhabitants thrived once more in harmony.

Word of reconciliation between once opposing races spread on ocean currents. Coastal youth embraced duties as sentinels, ensuring safe travels for all inhabitants throughout ancestral waters.

In reef-rich deltas, whale watching flourished as enlightened people witnessed migrations' grandeur. Eco-lodges hosted interspecies dialogues, fostering understanding between scholars of land and sea. Renewed guardians there guided encounters respecting boundaries.

Commerce upheld through sustainable enterprises honored the sacred home's gifts. Arts flourished depicting shared triumphs over strife through empathy. Songs carried news of flourishing pods, kindred relations restoring balance to the turning ages.

As seasons flowed, orations told of the visionary Songkeeper uplifting communities through unity. Her legacy endured in youth embracing their roles safekeeping the deep bonds connecting all people across the vast blue wilderness.

Zoe witnessed such hopeful lessons being raised to nourish new understanding. She sensed coming generations cultivated in such virtues of reverence, compassion and guardianship would birth eras where human and nature thrive as one ohana.

Renewed purpose echoed on as the deep magic of cooperation triumphed once more over division, ensuring ancestral tenants of interdependence nurture prosperous epochs to come.

HUNT FOR CLUES

Songs resonating upon coastal airs carried news of joyful migrations underway. Yet amongst whale clans traveled rumors of strange phenomena disturbing hidden caverns where ancestral ashes rested.

Seeking clarity, Zoe embarked with expert divers upon Songkeeper. Reaching remote calving grounds, they encountered Elder Orca Koti distressed by incidents disturbing sacred resting places.

Koti revealed unexplained sights amongst relics of past calamities recorded in corals and shells. Cave dwellers fled yet no beasts were seen, their possessions ransacked. "Spirits of chaos stir where order long prevailed," the elder said ominously.

Equipping submersibles, Zoe dove amongst reefs and kelp forests sensing ominous shifts. All fauna fled at her approach yet nothing visible disturbed the scenery. Only emptied shells remained where crustacean villages once thrived.

Exploring depths, Zoe's sub detected electromagnetic fluctuations matching no known creature. Infrared scans revealed phantom shapes disturbing silt like hurricanes beneath the waves.

Entering sacred caverns, Zoe witnessed relic shelves ransacked with precision, ashes of ancestors strewn without reverence. Yet no tracks disturbed the silt. Only a lingering feeling of disorienting wrongness permeated the hallowed places.

Consulting archives, scholars hypothesized evolutions in the abyss adapting to feast on electromagnetic signatures. Only the absence of matter could explain the phantom intrusions. Yet how did such immaterial beings disturb the physical world?

Seeking answers, Zoe lured one using a synthesized electromagnetic beacon. As it materialized, her subs closed in for samples, capturing its disorienting oscillation on film. Analysis showed it to be composed of exotic particles akin to hypothesized "dark matter".

Some believed such beings existed parallel to our realm, occasionally intersecting. Had subsurface shifts brought these two realities into confrontation? More answers were needed to determine impacts and ensure balance.

Consulting physicists, Zoe learned of theories positing multiple parallel dimensions intersecting at quantum levels. Subsurface seismic shifts may have stressed boundaries allowing "dark beings" passing through realms.

Seeking remedies, researchers developed technology translating electromagnetic patterns into visualized geometric forms for diplomacy. Projecting this before the caverns guided one cautiously inside.

There, Zoe communicated using synthesized song her people meant no harm if boundaries were respected. Though sensing disorientation from their realm's intersection, the being seemed amenable to order.

Experts determined with time, dimensional stresses would recede naturally if all inhabited spaces harmoniously. Zoe proposed boundaries designating caverns and electromagnetic fields "neutral zones" respected by all.

Dark beings agreed if provided frequencies guiding navigation. Coastal peoples committed maintaining sites undisturbed for ancestors of all kinds. Understanding emerged that despite basic natures, even disparate realms could find nonviolent coexistence.

News spread restoring balance with empathy's power over chaos. Zoe was heartened ancestral wisdom carried hope for future turns, as sentient races embraced duties upholding life-giving relationships across all domains.

Songs on the winds told of caverns and abyss restored to balance, as invisible kindred departed in amity. Coastal elders were heartened realization dawned all inhabitants, though differing in form or domain, mutually relied upon the sacred home.

In reef bridges teeming with life, cetacean scholars joined physicists weaving sonic narratives conveying humanity's peaceful explorations beyond observable realms. Such dialogues bridged gaps enabling new insights from outsiders' wisdoms.

Through innovation and compassion, frontiers once threatening became prosperous territories where sentient races flourished together in sacred trust. Children born would know their ohana extended even beyond customary boundaries.

Zoe witnessed such frontiers expanding cooperative spirit to nourish harmony in unknown turns of ages. She sensed in generations raised embracing diversity of all shapes and domains hope would blossom where fear once thrived.

Renewed in purpose, Songkeeper embarked bearing tales depicting triumphs of empathy over division. Ancient currents carried their spread throughout ancestral waters and unmapped borderlands, ensuring the deep magic of aloha would nourish flourishing epochs to come.

DISCOVERY AND DREAD

Spring gales ripped currents seething with change upon horizons. Yet beneath waves roiled tumults unknown disturbing kin long settled.

During patrols near volcanic vents, Zoe sensed tremors disquieting gelatinous beings dwelling where molten rivers birthed nourishment. Approaching, anguished cries echoed across the deep.

Arriving at the vents, Zoe witnessed chaos beyond experiences. Colossal forms thrashed amid plumes spewing wreckage as thermal towers collapsed, annihilating gardens choking with strange fruit.

Consulting specialists, they analyzed volcanic shifts rearranging submerged terrain. Yet these creatures behaved unlike any witnessed—amalgamations of diverse life driven by alien purpose. Their destructions appeared targeted, not circumstance.

Dreading revelations, Zoe captured samples for study. There analysts uncovered microscopic machines woven meticulously throughout flesh—biotechnology altering DNA with surgical precision. Their subjects had become instruments of subterfuge.

Analyzing the machines further, researchers identified advanced nanotechnology beyond known sphere's understanding. Specimens were blended with gelatinous and microbial polyps, rendering a killing juggernaut devoid of self-preservation.

Consulting sages, Zoe learned legends told of malign meddlers altering domains beyond mortal ken. Perhaps beings observing from beyond meddled in unfamiliar realms for sinister purposes unknown.

Equipping drones with sonic disruptors, Zoe aimed disabling frequencies at the hybrids. Their machines' mind control faltered, enabling the captured subjects' true natures emerging in anguished cries for help.

Releasing them from tanks, Zoe soothed with song and inspected for means undoing modifications. Specialists developed nanotech targeting parasitic alterations, restoring the victims to their original forms.

Word spread that malevolent watchers desecrated kin to further unfathomable ends. United, coastal peoples vowed combating aberrations through love defending all manifestations of life. Zoe vowed uncovering those behind this atrocity.

United peoples coordinated monitoring vent systems for further intrusions. Submersible fleets tracked volcanic fluctuations for anomalies indicating meddling. Patrols uncovered surgically modified lifeforms infesting newly formed thermal pools. Their machines acted as bioweapons annihilating communities establishing in the vents.

Using sonic deterrents, Zoe subdued their control while researchers developed nanobots excising infiltrating tech without harming hosts. Freed from parasitism, local fauna regrew in harmony with renewing hydrothermal springs.

Analyzing machines salvaged, experts identified resonant harmonic signatures matching none in known domains. Zoe hypothesized portals allowing passage between realms lay sealed in uncharted territories.

Charting coordinates of unknown origin,Songkeeper sailed beyond bordered seas. Crews descended discovering fissures woven with energy unlike nature's designs. Cracks between realities presented opportunity for manipulation.

Preparing submersibles, Zoe explored finding colossal lenses projecting energy altering quantum fields. A small vessel attended by aberrant life monitored inexplicable experiments. At last, those responsible were located.

Cloaking her vessel, Zoe observed infiltrators conducting quantum experiments splitting realities in the cracks. Their servants were abominations spliced from unknown domains, driven to desecrate all witnesses.

Consulting scholars, Zoe developed a communication system broadcasting appeals for parley in languages untainted by hostility. She approached the infiltrators' vessel requesting encounter through diplomacy.

To her surprise, they accepted via synthetic dialect. In the meeting, Zoe expressed locals sought only protecting their sacred home from harm. The infiltrators claimed observing without agency, guided by directives beyond their control.

Analyzing their vessel, experts determined lifeforms onboard were likewise engineered slaves. With aid, communications were established bypassing external controls. Freed individuals expressed desire departing the experiments in peace.

Uniting peoples then escorted the infiltrators to dimensional rifts, while nanites excised technologies coercing obedience. All parted mutually assured none would re-enter uncontrolled. Monitorings thereafter showed portals self-sealing permanently.

Through nonviolence and compassion and freeing minds from parasitic dominion, a calamitous confrontation was averted. Zoe took heart knowings such victories ensured hope for ages when all embrace inherent worth in life.

Songs of gratitude resonated throughout the depths. Coastal communities celebrated defenders of life who overcame the infiltrators through empathy instead of force.

In ceremony, Zoe and her crew were honored for upholding ancient wisdoms that divisions can be mended when all are seen as kindred. The mysterious manipulators departed in understanding, leaving none to disturb borders between worlds.

Scholars reflected on lessons learned. While some beings observed from afar, true guardians ensured all domains upheld equal regard for inhabitants, be they known or strange. Dominion over others could never justify harming life. In prophecy fires' glow, elders foretold generations raised witnessing such victories would pursue nonviolence resolutely in defense of their sacred home. Hope was kindled that through compassion's power over fear, even gravest perils could be overcome.

Renewed in spirit, Songkeeper sailed bearing messages far of this triumph fostering amity between disparate lives. Their spread ensured on turning currents that ages to come would see all sentient beings embrace mutual duties protecting life throughout the vast blue wilderness.

***

Chapter 09:

BREAKING TIDES

STORMS ON THE HORIZON

Songkeeper cruised amid elated songs celebrating life's victories. Yet troubling whispers arose upon horizons of change brewing overseas. Strange fleets pillaged distant reefs, clouding waters with debris.

Seeking clarity, Zoe sailed beyond bordered seas encountering crews from the east. Their captain spoke of homelands gripped by turmoil - resources dwindling as populations swelled. Leaders eyed ancestral waters for conquering to sate needs.

Consulting all who endured such strife, Zoe learned bringing balance required empathy, not conflict. "We must guide them to solutions ensuring all peoples' dignity," she told sailors. Despite impending threats, nonviolence would be their path.

Upon returning, Zoe shared sobering projections. Coastal communities mobilized navigating storms ahead through aloha's spirit. Elders tasked youth becoming emissaries fostering understanding with foreign realms.

Equipped with gifts and knowledge, they embarked bearing messages: "Through cooperation can needs be met without harming sacred life. Our home nourishes all respecting its gifts." Still, darkening storms brewed and awaited their approach.

Emissaries traveled beyond borders, greeting foreign captains speaking of hardships driving expansion. "Our peoples suffer as resources dwindle. We mean no violence, only ensuring dignity."

The sailors conveyed aloha's spirit embraced all life as sacred kin, advocating balance found through cooperation instead of conquest. Coastal communities welcomed sharing navigational skills, aquaculture techniques preserving biodiversity.

Some captains were moved, spreading messages of goodwill. But conflict profiteers sensed opportunities for domination claiming "resources belong to strongest." Their fleets swelled preparing to seize territories for private gains.

Conferring through messengers, Zoe proposed uniting all seeking balance through partnership. A pan-ocean delegation would navigate sustainable solutions ensuring dignity for populations while restoring depleted domains. Their proposal was accepted.

As fleets massed at borders, unity delegates from across regions convened exploring equitable resolutions. Through compassionate discussions seeking mutual benefit, accords were reached: depleted coasts would receive aid regenerating fisheries through non-exploitation.

In turn, foreign governments committed transitioning fleets to more noble purposes like resource monitoring, ceasing territorial ambitions threatening others' sovereignty.

News spread that through aloha and goodwill, empowering solutions were found avoiding catastrophe. Yet turbulent undercurrents endured as profiteers amassed fleets, disputing unity agreements obstructing conquests.

As tensions rose, Zoe proposed emissary voyages inviting all to coastal villages witnessing flourishing from nonviolence. Among people united in restoring life, even staunchest dissenters opened to compassion.

Among welcoming songs and dances, foreign captains beheld thriving interdependence where none exploited others. Children from all regions played as siblings, freed from prejudice. Witnessing aloha's fruits calmed militarized hearts long embroiled in division.

One captain swaying profiteers emerged transformed. "I saw how humanity finds dignity through unity, not domination. Resources sustained through respect becomes abundance for all." Returning, he urged leaders focus on sustainable partnership over conflict.

With unity swelling throughout lands, accord delegates collaborated transitioning fleets for purposes restoring depleted domains. Coastal communities shared expertise regrowing fisheries harmonizing with restored balances.

Storms of division receded as winds of cooperation swelled sails bearing all peoples' prosperity. Through aloha calming turbulent hearts, catastrophic collisions were averted, and generations found hope for epochs guided by empathy.

TESTING THE WATERS

While aloha rooted societies in balance, unrelenting profiteers conspired exploiting unrest. On turbulent currents whispers arrived from the north - once verdant coasts now poisoned by mercenaries draining toxic mines.

Native peoples suffered illnesses as polluted waters robbed them sustenance. In desperation, leaders launched flotillas pleading aid from coastal villages upholding life. Zoe volunteered emissaries ensuring dignified solutions.

Arriving, visitors found barren shores and sickened inhabitants. Mining syndicates dismissed pleas, pursuing toxic extraction unchecked. Analyzing waters, emissaries found pollution exceeding safe habitation.

"Through unity all peoples can restore this land," Zoe declared. Yet mercenaries threatened violence over interventions. After consulting elders and gathering allies, a resolution emerged.

Zoe proposed a pan-ocean convocation to address the plight. Representatives arrived bearing messages of aloha for the oppressed peoples. After learning of devastated livelihoods, open hearts prevailed.

Delegates collaborated envisioning restoration. Coastal experts agreed sharing aquaculture expertise regenerating fisheries as sustenance. Representatives from allied regions pledged material support for detoxification.

Yet polluters dismissed the plan, threatening mercenary raids on interferers. Tensions rose until a local elder spoke: "Through respect for all life, violence can be overcome. Let our people tell hard truths to open blind eyes, with compassion instead of anger."

The elder proposed a delegation visit mercenary leaders, sharing what pollution meant for native lives. "If seen as equal kin, even hardest hearts may soften to unity preserving dignity for all." Zoe affirmed nonviolence must be tried.

Marching with signs proclaiming "Aloha heals where hatred poisons," demonstrators approached mercenary zones. Sharing testimonies of devastated communities and pleading for the land's sake, oppression's grip began loosening.

Mercenary leaders watched demonstrators' plight with hardened eyes, dismissing pleas as obstruction. But among them, whispers of dissent emerged - some recalled ancestral ties to oppressed peoples now suffering needlessly.

Amid tension, one agent spoke: "Though called to serve money, within I know we all seek dignity. Our people also suffer when land is left desolate. There must be a path respecting livelihoods on both sides."

Hope kindled as unity's message stirred former allegiances to life. Leaders agreed meeting facilitators to explore equitable solutions sustaining all peoples. Through mediation tensions receded as conversations turned to restoration.

Coastal experts proposed phasing hazardous extraction, combining it with regenerating fisheries to employ all. Delegates pledged subsidies for alternative livelihoods during transition. Hardened faces softened witnessing a plan dignifying their fates too.

With pollution hotspots contained, healing land was celebrated by united peoples. Resources once wasted destructive extraction were redirected regenerating richness for communities. Where distrust once reigned, kinship's bonds flourished between formerly antagonized factions.

Horizons now brightened by restored balance. Through aloha challenging oppression peaceably, people found together the dignity denied by toxic profiteering. And in healing of the land, humanity's own restoration had begun.

News spread afar of the people's inspiring triumph prevailing over plunder through unity. In lands suffering similar crises, hope kindled from their example.

Requests arrived from realms blighted by unrest wishing for guidance navigating dissolution of inequalities through nonviolence. Zoe proposed establishing villages where all peoples injured by divisions could commune finding mutual empowerment.

The Islands of Awakening welcomed communities committing to restore justice through respect, not retaliation. There, indigenous leaders counseled utilizing ancestral wisdom resolving conflicts cooperatively. Representatives from allied regions aided regenerating livelihoods.

Graduates of these villages embarked as emissaries, sharing hard-won lessons fostering understanding between opposing sides. Their messages of aloha took root calming tensions across borders, as marginalized peoples regained agency through unity instead of fighting alone.

Where fear and greed once profited dividing populations, caring for neighbors prospered in restored dignity for all. Forests and fisheries revived under cooperative stewardship. With basic needs secured non-exploitatively, creativity nourished blossoming cultures.

Horizons remained bright, with seeds of compassion outplanting antipathy's dying roots throughout lands. Through lessons of aloha, more peoples awakened to humanity's shared stake in upholding life.

Generations nurtured in awakened villages embraced diversity as family, not division. Youth from all backgrounds learned as siblings the magic of compassion overcoming oppression.

Graduates established Unity Academies throughout lands, mentoring future leaders committed to balance through respecting life and cultural traditions. There, students studied ancestral wisdoms resolving conflicts cooperatively.

They embarked across oceans sharing lessons regenerating depleted domains. By fostering pride in cultural strengths alongside empathy for differences, fragmented societies reunited in shared stewardship of ancestral waters.

Forests and fisheries revived across domains under reverence for nature's gifts, sustaining all peoples with abundance. With livelihoods secured nonviolently, creativity blossomed as cultures flourished in restored dignity.

Witnessing harmony's roots taking hold, Zoe's heart swelled sensing coming ages guided by empathy. She took Songkeeper bearing aloha's triumphs far to kindle hope that unity's magic would blossom throughout humankind, and Earth's blessings be sustained for turning ages.

RAGING SEAS

While unity spread renewal across lands, dark undercurrents gathered strength. Among remnants of profiteers deposed from polluted realms, resentment festered against peoples restoring balance nonviolently.

Conspiring in shadowed ports, these dissenters formed Syndicates of exploitation. Through cunning manipulation and shows of force, they infiltrated foreign governments with promises of riches from unrestricted extraction.

Lands where unity once overcame devastation fell sway to new tyranny. Forests and fisheries suffered second wounding as populations were pitted against each other. Coastal communities received calls for aid from oppressed peoples.

Zoe offered mediation to resolve tensions before erupting into open conflict. "Through empathy we overcame plunderers before - unity can prevail again if all parties' dignity is respected." Hope held nonviolence might quell rising storms.

Arriving, delegates found lands turbulent as exploitation sowed unrest. Syndicate puppets criminalized unity's advocates, spurring dissent into chaos. Tribal factions clashed while ecosystems collapsed under unfettered activity.

Seeing peoples' desperation, Zoe's heart sank knowing nonviolence alone may not calm raging seas. What strategies could restore balance with tyranny threatening very lives and shelter compassion's flames from extinguishing?

Convening peoples to surface united purpose amid division, Zoe spoke: "Within each community lies power overcoming oppression through aloha, not weapons. Let shared dreams of dignity guide us."

Calls went out summoning representatives across factions to communes restoring trust. There, tribal elders soothed tensions by honoring cultural strengths alongside shared hopes. Youth bonded beyond divides through restoring forests as collective heritage.

Reunited, participants forged accords for cooperative stewardship managing resources sustainably. Mechanisms ensured fair dispute resolution to isolate profiteers' manipulation. Plans took shape transitioning exploited lands back to native guardianship.

Yet Syndicate governors struck back threatening violence against "rebels". Zoe appealed for non-escalation through open dialogue, but doors remained shut. Factions prepared clashing while youth sought peaceful paths.

Among them, a tribal daughter spoke: "Our people wish dignity, not fighting. If our leaders meet as kin beyond walls dividing them, understanding may emerge." After prayers for wisdom, a delegation braved approaching adversaries.

The delegation approached Syndicate command bearing gifts and songs of unity. "We see your people also desire dignity - let us seek it together."

Governors met coldly, refusing cooperation. But among them dissent emerged as some recalled ancestral ties now severed by manipulation. "Must we betray kinship for fleeting power?" one whispered.

Through respectful insistence, dissent spread. The tribal daughter shared their vision: restored lands managed by native guardians in balanced coexistence with all peoples. "Power found through empathizing, not dominating others."

Cracks widened in allegiance to oppression as leaders contemplated dignity for all. One governor spoke: "You appeal to parts of self long suppressed. Give us time in silence to reflect on kinship's call over resentment."

The people fasted and prayed, hoping empathy might touch even stoniest of hearts. And in solitude, governors awakened remembering relationships once nurtured, now poisoned by power ambition. A message arrived: "Return - we wish resolving divisions as family."

Reuniting, former adversaries embraced in tears. Accords were forged for transitional self-governance and rehabilitation of lands, bringing balance and prosperity for all peoples.

With unity's triumph over division, restored lands flourished under reverence for nature's blessings. Tribal communities collaborated cultivating forests, rewarding all peoples' stewardship with bountiful harvests.

The Communes of Kinship welcomed all wishing to commune finding unity amid diversity. There, folk from across the lands lived as ohana, students learning respect for cultural identities alongside shared hope for our relations' dignity.

Graduates established Unity Academies to nurture future leaders in balancing progress with tradition. Throughout forests, their songs and dances nurtured pride in ancestry while fostering connection across borders.

Where manipulation once exploited differences, shared celebration of life's gifts strengthened diverse peoples' bonds. With basic needs satisfied through cooperation instead of competition, creativity blossomed as communities supported each other's flourishing.

Horizons remained bright, empathy's roots taking hold to sustain humankind and Earth in balance. Though darkness lingers, each act of aloha chips away tyranny while nurturing tomorrow's stewards. Zoe took heart seeing unity's seeds spreading humanity's reawakening to our shared stake in life.

Aboard Songkeeper, Zoe sailed bearing their triumphs afar to ignite hope against all oppressions. Future generations raised embracing diversity as ohana would safekeep gifts bequeathed by ancestors, for turning ages guided by compassion.

THE DARKEST HOUR

While unity spread renewal restoring balance, dissent festered in dark reaches. Remnants of profiteering syndicates vowed revenge against "traitors" collaborating with "enemies."

In shadow ports they conspired new atrocities exploiting lands weakened by past divisions. Poisonous whispers spread manipulating disgruntled factions with promises of riches from unrest. instability spread like wildfire across borders.

As lands descended into turmoil, urgent pleas arrived from oppressed peoples. Zoe offered mediation, hoping aloha could soothe tensions before erupting into catastrophic conflict. But arriving, a scene of horror awaited—entire villages annihilated in mercenary raids.

Survivors wept, recounting unspeakable atrocities commanded by terror gangs ravaging the region. "They spare no one—even children are butchered if resisting," cried a weary mother clutching her dead babe. Zoe's heart sank at the darkness humanity was capable of.

Despite anguish, she vowed staying true to nonviolence. "Through empathy alone can the darkness be overcome." But could unity's message still reach blackened hearts intent on sowing further mayhem? The darkest of tests had begun.

Despite the horror, Zoe remained steadfast in nonviolence. "Even in darkness, a spark of light remains in every soul."

She approached survivors consoling the grieving. "Vengeance will spread only more suffering. Let us find justice through respecting each other's humanity."

Together they planned humanitarian relief, sharing whatever comfort was possible. Word spread summoning volunteers across lands still at peace.

Supplies arrived as communities rebuilt sheltering the displaced. But gang leaders mocked these "naïve fools," threatening further bloodshed against "traitors to true power." Darkness seemed poised to swallow all light.

Then a orphan spoke: "If we appeal their lost kinship, may hatred's grip loosen." Zoe agreed, assembling a delegation to approach mercenaries under flag of parley.

Greeting them holding aloft the children's artwork of hope, she said "Even your victims see humanity in you. Let us forge understanding as family, to end this vicious cycle."

The hardened men scoffed—but among them, whispers emerged of forgotten bonds to the oppressed. "Must we betray ancestral ties for coins and violence?" one said. A glimmer of hope remained.

The mercenary leaders met coldly at first, but cracks emerged in allegiance to terror as whispers spread of kinship long forgotten.

One spoke: "You appeal to ancestors' memory of relationship. Though darkness clouds my vision, let me gaze on humanity's faces and reflect."

The delegation shared meals, opening hearts amid shared moments of laughter and tears. Stories stirred faint memories of unity in leaders numbed by violence.

In solitude, one gazed at innocent faces and wept--recalling his own childhood and victims' pleas. A message came: "Return at dawn--darkness lifts and kinship calls me home."

At the fated hour, they arrived to find arms laid down and oppressors embracing survivors as family. Vowing redemption through rebuilding what was destroyed, darkness' final stronghold crumbled at aloha's insistence.

With tyranny's end, restored lands prospered through cooperation across borders. Communities nurtured orphans who would grow raising future generations empowered by empathy. Forests revived under reverence for life as a shared inheritance.

Unity prevailed through compassion's flame kept burning even in darkness' depths. Zoe took heart that no shadow, however deep, could extinguish humanity's spark for relationship.

***

Chapter 10:

AN OCEAN'S VOICE

AFTER THE STORM

After the storms were calmed through aloha's power reviving kinship's bonds, the lands entered an era of renewal. Communities proliferated where peoples of diverse backgrounds lived as ohana, nurturing dignity through empathy.

Forests, waters and cultures blossomed under reverence for nature's gifts as a sacred inheritance. With basic needs secured cooperatively instead of through competition, creativity flourished as communities supported each others' development.

Yet distant shores still called Zoe seeking unity's guidance. She embarked once more aboard Songkeeper, bearing aloha's songs across the seas. Weeks passed journeying territories emerging from exploitation's wounds.

One dawn, a pod of humpback whales appeared dancing alongside their vessel. Zoe was intrigued - rarely did such majestic beings interact so intimately unless summoning aid. Through melodies the whales conveyed urgent pleas from lands wounded by industrializing.

Zoe pledged responding. Following the pod's lead, shorelines materialized bleak and barren where lush rainforests once flourished. Logging syndicates devastated the realm, sowing unrest as peoples' ways of life were destroyed.

Arriving, Zoe found lands torn and tensions high. Logging trucks terrorized villages as forests fell at an alarming rate. Industry puppeteers pitted ethnic groups against each other to obscure true roots of suffering.

Delegates greeted her coldly until the whales sang ancestral poems conveying people's shared hopes. Cracks formed in hardened facades as memories stirred of relationship before discord.

That evening communities gathered by the sea. Elders soothed divisions speaking of cultural gifts as shared inheritance if preserved with balance. Youth bonded beyond divides through play as water-kin lifted spirits with revelry.

In the whispering pines Zoe counseled reunited factions: "Your dignity and nature's gifts are one. Rebuild trust cooperatively so industry extracts no further price in broken kinship or scars on the land."

Leaders embraced plans for stewardship with sustainability and fairness. Techniques ensured transparent governance isolating corruption. Restoration hopes emerged from ashes of destruction.

Yet puppet bosses struck back threatening further brutality if resisting. Could nonviolence prevail against plunderers deaf to life's cries? The whales sang for courage in their reply.

Factions prepared for the worst, yet Zoe appealed once more for open-hearted dialogue. "Through respecting each other's humanity, understanding can overcome even deepest mistrust."

Greeting officials holding gifts of aloha, she shared peoples' vision: stewardship through revering nature as provider for all generations. "With open hands and ears, find dignity for all."

Some leaders scoffed, but among them wavered those recalling life before greed severed bonds. "Must we betray kinship itself for fleeting gain?" one said privately.

In solitude, logging chieftains heard the whales' lament and saw peoples' suffering. Awoken were memories of relationships built through empathy, not power over others.

A message came declaring: "Return - we wish resolving divisions as 'ohana should." Reuniting, former adversaries embraced, and accords were formed for restoring balance through cooperation instead of competition.

Forests revived through respecting the land as inheritance. With basic needs achieved cooperatively, creativity flourished as communities supported all peoples' well-being. Light returned to the horizon.

Yet dark shadows remained. How could unity ensure future ages embrace stewardship guided by compassion, not exploitation's injuries? The whales sang for wisdom to safeguard life's gifts.

With unity prevailing over division, restored lands thrived in balance. Tribal communities collaborated cultivating rainforests and rewarding all peoples' care through nature's bounty.

Elders founded Schools of Kinship where folk of every background lived as 'ohana, embracing their cultural identities while cultivating respect for others.

There students learned treating land and water with reverence as a sacred trust. Graduates established Sanctuaries along waterways welcoming peoples seeking refuge from exploitation's divisions.

Throughout the realm, song and dance nurtured ancestral pride while strengthening bonds across communities. Hand in hand with the whales, youth played among waves honoring oceans' gifts.

Leaders ensured mechanisms for sustaining democracy, enshrining dignity and Earth's well-being in governance. Corruption found no foothold where peoples prioritized one another's prosperity.

With cooperation satisfying needs, dreams flourished as communities supported each other's growth. Forests and cultures revived, diversity renewing the landscape. Hope spread on waves of aloha danced with the whales' reply. Horizons remained bright, yet shadows linger where greed persists. How could empathy's roots take deepest hold, safeguarding gifts bequeathed by ancestors for turning ages to come?

CHANGING PERSPECTIVES

With restored lands prospering through unity, Zoe embarked anew sharing aloha's message of relationship. Following ancestral songs, her vessel journeyed uncharted archipelagos where peoples seldom interacted beyond their shores.

Arriving at a isolated chain, Zoe encountered suspicious sentries. "Strangers disrupt balance - depart, or defend yourselves!" Wishing peace, she conveyed through sign respecting their autonomy.

Intrigued by novel craft, the islanders welcomed learning visitors' ways provided balances theirs. Exchanges nurtured understanding as communities exchanged traditions not just goods.

Days passed joyfully until elders noticed youth vanishing into forest daily. Following, Zoe glimpsed them playing with creatures never before described - tiny folk speaking intelligibly yet dwelling invisible to modern lenses.

The children conveyed the spirits' plight - their realm shrinking as outsider technology scrambled magic. Zoe pondered how empowering the 'little ones' with dignity and partnership, not domination, could nourish both realms.

Elders were wary, yet children's delight with their playmates stirred faint memories of previous ways. A council was called under a banyan centuries old.

There, ancestors' voices whispered through branches urging listening with fairness to all. Spirits emerged sharing tales of stewardship when realms co-existed in balance.

Toku, a wise sprite, proposed respecting each realm's gifts through unity instead of separation. "Our magic nourishes your sacred sites unseen; your sharing sustains wandering souls."

After reflection, elders agreed trying partnership guided by empathy, not power over one another. Messengers among youth and sprites strengthened ties as communities collaborated.

Where outsiders saw only what modern tools revealed, islanders embraced multisensory perception honoring ancestors witnessing unseen lives enriching their own. Diverse perspectives fostered greater wellbeing for all.

Zoe took heart such small openings could foster outsized renewal when approached with aloha. She embarked bearing their story further, hoping diminished views of "the other" might begin enlarging.

With restored trust between realms, invisible spirits again danced joyfully as islanders embraced fuller awareness. Children developed keen abilities perceiving worldlights brightening interactions.

Word spread summoning fellow seekers to observe flourishing of open-hearted ways. Scholars arrived yet clung to age of so-called progress severing ways from means. "Savages must modernize or perish," some claimed.

Zoe invited courteous dialogue. "All peoples evolve cooperatively - none predetermined to vanish. Let realities stir understanding beyond preconceptions."

Still some saw only confirmations of biases. But open minds accompanied Zoe encountering sprites, sensing truths beyond narrow teachings. Witnessing unity's gifts firsthand expanded their perceptions.

One scholar wrote home pondering: "If we often know parts of others not whole beings, how reshape views broadening what we see?"

News reached lands recovering empathy's roots, summoning communities worldwide honoring ancestors amid changes. Delegations arrived embracing islanders as kin, diversity flourishing where aloha prevailed.

Zoe took heart perspectives changing shape community bonds. Equipped with open eyes and ears, our shared human 'ohana could nourish differences as richness for all. Renewal was only beginning.

With restored trust nurturing diverse communities, Zoe embarked once more spreading aloha's promise of unity. Following ancestral songs, her vessel journeyed realms recovering from exploitation's divisions.

Arriving remote shores, she found peoples clutching to fading traditions amid turmoil. Generations lost purpose as land and cultural practices were disturbed for outsider profits.

Desperate leaders accepted promises of cash before realizing sacred gifts could not be bought or replaced. Now youth grasped at illusions of modernity, forgetting ancestors' wisdom of balance.

Gaining trust, Zoe shared hopeful accounts of cooperation overcoming even deepest wounds. Through empathy and reverence for diversity, unity's roots took hold where cynicism once reigned.

Elders sensed faint memories stirring of empowerment through relationship, not domination. Youth curious about origins beyond monetary myths accompanied Zoe encountering sprites playfully enacting ancestral tales.

Witnessing invisible lives enriched their community expanded perspectives. Grudges dissolved as shared hopes emerged for partnership guided by aloha, not dependency.

Through exchanges nurturing cultural revival, understanding blossomed that none need vanish if embracing shared destinies. With support networks of trusted allies, all peoples could evolve cooperatively.

Renewed, the community pledged nurturing such relationships where empathy and dignity for diversities flourished as richness for all. Dark clouds continued lifting from unity's horizon.

With awakened spirit of aloha restoring hope, the community mobilized revitalizing traditions. Elders and youth alike dove into forests rediscovering medicinal plants and crafts.

Children eagerly assisted sprites enacting dances among wildflowers come alive with stories. Bonds formed between realms unseen and seen, empowering invisibles to quietly aide sacred sites unseen by modern eyes.

Scholars from afar arrived yet clung to notions of "progress" demanding assimilation. Some saw only obstacles confirming biases, not realities widening views. But open-minded learned much experiencing revitalization firsthand.

One wrote home reflecting: "If we embrace others as relatives not competitions, how does collaboration over domination nourish community?"

Word spread summoning gatherings celebrating restored ties between peoples and lands. Delegations arrived from afar embracing revived culture as shared roots, diversity flourishing where aloha prevailed.

With kinship networks of trusted allies emerged, exploitation could find no foothold where community prioritized well-being. Renewed in purpose, youth chose revival over dependency, confident ancestors' wisdom sufficed for generations to come.

Hope continued its journey on waves of aloha nourishing hidden buds of connection between even most disparate beings. Transformation's depths were being navigated by open eyes witnessing shared humanity.

A WHISPER HEARD AROUND THE WORLD

With lands flourishing through aloha restoring relationships, Zoe embarked bearing witness further. Following waves carrying hopes for unity, her vessel journeyed to continental shores recovering from exploitation's wounds.

Arriving a vast region, Zoe found peoples suffering divisions sown by outsiders seizing territories. Generations lost homes and purpose as lands were taken and communities torn asunder.

Gaining trust, elders shared painful histories and youth expressed discontent with empty lives. Yet beneath cynicism lingered faint memories of empowerment through cooperation.

Zoe conveyed hopeful accounts of lands overcoming even deepest injuries by embracing shared fates. Through empathy and reverence for diversity, unity's roots took hold where desolation once reigned.

Intrigued, many attended gatherings to hear more. There, sprites and visitors from flourishing isles recounted witnessing invisible lives enriching communities. How perspectives expanded empowering all peoples.

At the gatherings, conversations deepened between former adversaries. Memories stirred of empowerment through relationship binding communities as family.

Youths accompanied Zoe into forests where sprites playfully enacted ancestors' teachings of balance. Witnessing invisible lives nourishing sacred places enlarged spectators' perspectives.

Scholars arrived to study, but some clung to notions of inevitable demise for "primitive" ways. Through respectful debate with open-minded counterparts, perceptions began shifting.

One wrote reflecting, "If we embrace others' humanity beyond surface traits, how does mutual recognition nourish community where dominance now divides?"

Heartened, elders proposed restoring ancestral homelands by nurturing forests and traditions. Youth mobilized across divisions inspired by tales of cultural revival and dignity.

Kinship networks emerged sustaining revived practices and knowledge-sharing without dependency. Green shoots broke ground where cynicism once took root, empowered communities' well-being priority over illusions.

Seeing flourishing partnerships, outsiders realized forced assimilation stripped peoples' richness. Talk began of reconciling past harms through restoration and relationship, not domination or reparations alone.

Hope continued spreading its message of unity through exchanges empowering everyone. Transformation blossomed as aloha took deeper root.

With kinship networks supporting revival, diverse communities thrived empowered. Youth embraced ancestors' wisdom, confident traditions sufficed generations hence.

Renewed lands summoned wider gatherings celebrating cultural rebirth. Delegations arrived from afar embracing diversity as shared heritage. Hope spread on waves of aloha bonded between peoples.

Word reached distant capitals of transformed relationships overcoming society's oldest divides. Leaders reconsidered policies sundering ties between peoples and homelands and reflected on paths toward restored justice.

Grassroots movements catalyzed by aloha's message advocated respecting sovereignty and diversity for flourishing of all. Once-disparate citizens recognized shared fates and mobilized together.

Changes began as communities received authority governing lands, languages and self-determination and forming councils for mutual support. Revitalized, peoples prospered empowered through reverence for difference as richness.

Zoe sailed bearing witness far, certain humanity's awakening was only deepening its roots. Through aloha's power of relationship, even deepest cynicism could evolve toward empathy nurturing shared well-being.

Transformation's deepest waters were yet being navigated, yet on its journey hope remained steadfast - that open eyes may see our shared lifeblood and roots strengthen bonds between all people and lands for turning ages to come.

THEIR CHAMPION

With renewed lands prospering in balance, Zoe embarked bearing aloha's message of unity ever wider. Centuries voyaging Earth's seas awakened in her remembrance of ancient duties as champion of oceans and all their relations.

Arriving great gatherings celebrating restoration, she witnessed youth empowered learning traditions ensuring wellsprings of wisdom. Diverse communities thrived recognized in sovereignty, reviving ways ancients bequeathed as gifts.

Yet whispers reached Zoe from deep currents - industrious newcomers' actions threatened offshore life with unforeseen changes. She journeyed investigations, alarmed by impacts disrupting ancient songs within waves.

Surfacing among peaceful folk harvesting bounty with respect, she shared concern for more-than-human kin. Elders convened considering impacts upon sacred trust to safeguard all for ages hence.

At gatherings, Zoe conveyed oceans' calls through elders' tongues, stirring faint memories of duty as stewards. Youth accompanied her witnessing vibrant coral songs nourished by unseen spirits of place.

Open minds grasped impacts jeopardizing sustenance and spirit worlds intertwined with waters. But some outsiders dismissed ancients as "primitive" and denied connection between ways of living and offshore worlds.

Through respectful dialogue comparing observations, perspectives shifted. "If we embrace complex relationships woven through all lives, how does restoring balance nourish communities?" one scholar reflected.

Inspired communities mobilized traditional arts aiding habitats and restoring balance. Councils formed across seafaring peoples for mutual aid safeguarding oceans through aloha's reverence for diversity.

Word spread summoning dialogues to share solutions strengthening ties between lands and waves. Delegations arrived embracing oceans as arteries of life coursing through all lands and peoples.

United in stewardship, communities worldwide awakened ancestral songs resonating within every pulse. Hope rose on mighty currents that together humanity could safeguard gifts bequeathed through aloha's power of relationship, for generations sailing yet to be.

Zoe's ancient duty found renewal as champion nurturing restoration. Earth's first songs of unity would continue reverberating across all lands, lives and lineages, binding our shared 'ohana.

With oceans' wellbeing prioritized through relationship, thriving communities monitored changing tides. Elders' keen perceptions detected impacts intensifying from afar requiring united response.

Summoning gatherings, Zoe conveyed urgency to safeguard sustenance for all peoples. Delegations arrived committed to harmony yet perplexed by pervasive transformations disrupting ancient songs.

Through respectful dialogue bridging views, outsider and community scholars compared notes. Patterns emerged between industrial materials poisoning life ways from sources beyond any land.

Youth proposed traditional arts aiding habitats be shared worldwide inspiring broader restoration. Councils coordinated international networks supporting communities on frontlines absorbing heaviest impacts.

Hope rose on swellings of unity resisting defeatism. Through reverence for difference as shared heritage, could humanity navigate looming crisis where shortsightedness once divided?

New currents stirred souls toward solutions strengthening ties between all lands, lives and lineages. Leaders reflected on policies privileging profits over relationship with waters nourishing communities for ages past and future.

Citizens mobilized pressuring leaders to overhaul destructive ways, recognizing shared fates. Grassroots movements flourished catalyzed by aloha prioritizing wellbeing of generations yet sailing.

Changes were set in motion as communities worldwide awakened ancestral roles as stewards, governing lands and seas flourishing together in balance. Zoe took heart- humanity's revolution was only deepening roots.

With communities empowered in protecting the life-giving oceans as kuleana, swift changes swept the lands. Grassroots uprisings pressured leaders to transition industrial policies destroying balance and sovereignty.

After centuries of division, global assemblies formed with delegates from all shores united through aloha's spirit of relationship. Councils coordinated shifting economies grounded in stewardship of Earth's gifts for all future generations.

Resources were redirected supporting frontline communities bearing heaviest consequences. Ancestral ecological knowledge was shared far and wide, reviving ancient songs of the sea in souls worldwide.

Where cynicism and denial once reigned, open-eyed youth took charge nurturing restoration. They journeyed spread aloha's message of unity and empowerment through diversity far beyond any shores.

Zoe witnessed humanity's awakening with joy, confident the tides had turned for healingEarth's wounds and safeguarding life's wellspring for all the turns of world to come. Though more work lay ahead, hope's voice was sounding clear - through relationship could even greatest threats be overcome.

With Earth's diverse peoples standing as one 'ohana, the ancient duty of stewardship had found new life. From poles to equator, skies to abyss, the first song of unity and empowerment through diversity would forever resound.

And so, with lands and seas flourishing once more in balance through aloha, Zoe's long championing drew to a close. Her mission was renewed in all carrying forth Earth's gifts in reciprocity and care for the generations yet to be.

***

SUMMARY

The story follows Zoe, a teenage girl who lives near the coast and has always felt deeply connected to whales. She believes she can understand their songs and communicate with them, though no one else understands her gift.

One morning, Zoe is awakened by a distress call from the whales. She hears a pod of humpback whales singing for help and races out to locate them. With some convincing, Zoe gets her mother to take her out on their boat. Following the song, they find the pod entangled in fishing nets, injured and exhausted. Zoe helps guide the Coast Guard to their rescue. In the process, she forms a close bond with the whales, especially a young calf she helps free from netting wrapped around its tail.

This proves to the town that Zoe's connection is real. However, the rescue also attracts the ire of the poachers who laid the illegal fishing gear. They threaten revenge on Zoe and the whales. Not long after, Zoe spots the poachers harassing the pod in speedboats. She bravely intervenes, even setting the water on fire to separate the whales and drive the men off.

From this point, Zoe dedicates herself to advocating for the pod's protection. With the help of marine biologists, she works to gather evidence against the organized poaching ring. Zoe spends extensive time bonding with the whales to learn their behaviors and songs, sharing insights to help the researchers. During this time, she develops especially close relationships within the pod.

However, the pod is still threatened as the poachers go underground. Then one morning 5 whales are discovered missing. Zoe is distraught but remains determined. Drawing on her connection, she is able to sense where the whales are being held captive. In a dramatic raid, the abandoned marine warehouse is stormed and the stolen whales are rescued while the poachers are arrested.

Order is restored to the ocean, but Zoe remains committed to the pod. She continues strengthening her ability to communicate with them and advocating for their safety, proving herself a true ally and voice for whales.

ABOUT THE AUTHOR

Mustafa A. Nejem is a maritime visionary with a captain's heart and an island soul. In his island home, the sea's love, sailing's legacy, and leadership's flame passed down through generations with pride and glory. He is a skilled navigator of words, charting a course through the vast ocean of knowledge. With his expertise and passion , he guide readers towards prosperous shores, unveiling the secrets of maritime life and business success in concise and captivating prose.

www.ingramcontent.com/pod-product-compliance
Lightning Source LLC
Chambersburg PA
CBHW080851120626
46546CB00008B/2778